a–z of

C000177073

professional keywords

Every field of practice has its own methods, terminology, conceptual debates and landmark publications. The *Professional Keywords* series expertly structures this material into easy-reference A to Z format. Focusing on the ideas and themes that shape the field, these books are designed both to guide the student reader and to refresh practitioners' thinking and understanding.

Available now

Mark Doel and Tim Kelly: *A–Z of Groups and Group Work*
David Garnett: *A–Z of Housing*
Jon Glasby and Helen Dickinson: *A–Z of Interagency Working*
Richard Hugman: *A–Z of Professional Ethics*
Glenn Laverack: *A–Z of Health Promotion*
Glenn Laverack: *A–Z of Public Health*
Jeffrey Longhofer: *A–Z of Psychodynamic Practice*
Neil McKeganey: *A–Z of Addiction and Substance Misuse*
Steve Nolan and Margaret Holloway: *A–Z of Spirituality*
Marian Roberts: *A–Z of Mediation*
David Wilkins, David Shemmings and Yvonne Shemmings:
    A–Z of Attachment

a–z of
attachment

David Wilkins

David Shemmings

and

Yvonne Shemmings

 palgrave

First published 2015 by
PALGRAVE

Palgrave in the UK is an imprint of Macmillan Publishers Limited, registered in England, company number 785998, of 4 Crinan Street, London N1 9XW.

Palgrave Macmillan in the US is a division of St Martin's Press LLC, 175 Fifth Avenue, New York, NY 10010.

Palgrave is a global imprint of the above companies and is represented throughout the world.

Palgrave® and Macmillan® are registered trademarks in the United States, the United Kingdom, Europe and other countries.

ISBN: 978–1–137–00826–8

This book is printed on paper suitable for recycling and made from fully managed and sustained forest sources. Logging, pulping and manufacturing processes are expected to conform to the environmental regulations of the country of origin.

A catalogue record for this book is available from the British Library.

A catalog record for this book is available from the Library of Congress.

Printed in China.

contents

introduction and
'how to' guide

Of all the various theories of human development, attachment theory is arguably the most popular amongst health and social care professionals and one of the best supported in terms of research and evidence. In this book, we discuss many of the most important concepts from attachment theory in an accessible and novel format for the busy professional. Using an 'A to Z' layout, one could say that we have written a flexible, 'postmodern' book, enabling the reader to find their own structure within the material. We also offer a 'guided tour', should one be needed, with the inclusion of frequent cross-referencing between the different sections (any words that are italicized within the book refer to a discrete section of that name). We hope this book will prove useful as a reference guide for those who need quickly and easily to access some brief but contemporary information on specific attachment-related concepts. Additionally, we hope the book will prove especially helpful to health and social care professionals who may have a basic understanding of attachment theory and who want to develop their knowledge further.

Although the A–Z nature of the book enables readers to engage with the material in whichever way they find most useful, in this introductory chapter we aim to do two things: firstly, to set out the basics of attachment theory to provide a context for what follows and, secondly, to identify a number of key themes within attachment theory – such as 'adult attachment' or 'attachment research' – and then provide a list of the most useful sections to read in order to gain a more developed understanding of each theme. The themes we have identified are fluid, in the sense that some of the A–Z sections may be relevant to more than one of the themes. Again, this reflects the flexible nature of the book and enables the reader to essentially create his or her own text. So, for example, one of the themes we have identified is 'attachment patterns and behaviour' and this includes sections on secure attachment, insecure attachment, avoidant attachment and ambivalent-resistant attachment. However, we have also identified a wider theme of 'attachment and children', which includes these four sections plus a number of others. We do not assume that many readers will work their way through the book from cover to cover, from A to Z; neither would we expect the reader to work through every theme. Rather, we suggest selecting the themes or sections that are most useful or applicable for your area of practice and hope that you then find the cross-referencing useful as a guide to further exploration, in whatever direction you prefer.

In addition, we will also discuss in this introduction the application of attachment theory in practice. Given the popularity of attachment theory within many and various fields of health and social care, it is not surprising that much has been written on this topic already. What may be more surprising, however, is how little research there has been on 'how' health and (in particular) social care professionals actually use attachment theory in practice, as opposed to recommendations for how they 'could' or 'should' use it (see Wilkins, 2014). Thus, we want to discuss – outside of any particular section – our views on the use of attachment theory in practice in broad terms and on how we think this book in particular might inform the reader's practice.

attachment theory – the basics

Attachment theory is concerned with the giving and receiving of care and protection, and how children and adults are able to use their close, primary relationships as a source of security (or not). In developing these ideas, John Bowlby, the originator of attachment theory, put forward the hypothesis that young children, when distressed or anxious, will tend to seek physical and emotional comfort from a familiar adult, someone who Bowlby described as the child's attachment figure. For example, a two-year-old child, upon hearing a sudden, loud noise may feel scared and run towards his mother, father or some other attachment figure. Bowlby described this kind of behaviour, that is, anything the child might do in order to achieve the goal of 'felt security', as 'attachment behaviour' and the child's use of the attachment figure as a 'safe haven', that is, someone to whom the child can turn for comfort and protection during times of heightened anxiety. Based on how the child's attachment figures respond to their attachment behaviour, Bowlby hypothesized that different children would form different kinds of 'internal working models' of close relationships. As the child grows older, s/he uses these internal working models as a way of predicting the most likely responses from their attachment figures and to organize their own attachment behaviour so as to maximize the chances of receiving a comforting response. One note of caution is that the expression of attachment behaviour on the part of the child does not necessarily indicate that the adult to whom the behaviour is directed is in reality an attachment figure. It may be that they are; it may be that they are not (but may become one) or it may be that they are not (and will not become one). Therefore, it is not unexpected that, especially when young, a distressed child might exhibit attachment behaviour to any available adult in the hopes of receiving some form of comfort and protection. However, it is also the case that if the child has formed an attachment relationship – and almost all children will begin doing so between the ages of 6 and 12 months – then they will preferentially seek out one of their actual attachment figures when distressed or anxious, in preference to any other adult.

As attachment research developed and as noted above, it became apparent that the attachment behaviour of different children could be seen as representing different kinds of *internal working models* of close relationships. Some children seemed to develop a model in which their attachment figure is consistently and sensitively available for them (these children had a secure attachment relationship with the carer). Other children, however, developed a model in which their attachment figure was either consistently unavailable or inconsistently available (these children were seen as having an 'insecure attachment relationship' with the carer). At this point, it is important to note that attachment behaviours and internal working models are linked to specific relationships. They do not reflect an inherent feature of the child. Thus, it is inaccurate to refer to a 'secure child' or an 'insecure child'; it is more correct to think of a 'secure (or insecure) attachment relationship' existing between the child and a specific attachment figure. For example, imagine a child with two attachment figures – the child may experience the first attachment figure as sensitive and consistently available and thus, the child may display secure attachment behaviour with them. But the same child may experience their other attachment figure as consistently insensitive and unavailable, so they may display different attachment behaviour with this second attachment figure. As they get older, when their attachment system is activated, children tend to respond to others in the way that they do with the adult they spend most of their time with – they 'hardwire' to that person. The exception occurs if a child is being maltreated by a parent/carer. In these circumstances they will tend to develop their internal working model to the abuser, even though they may spend less time in their presence.

As this research tradition developed, it also became clear that some children, especially those with secure attachment relationships, were also more confident when in the presence of the attachment figure with whom they felt secure, and hence were more able to leave that attachment figure and explore the wider environment. Conversely, children who felt less secure tended to be less confident in leaving their attachment figure to explore the world around them. This observation is referred to as the child's use of their attachment figure as a 'secure base' from which to explore.

So far, we have briefly described the first fundamental aspect of attachment theory – the child's attachment relationship with one or more attachment figures. Caregiving describes the reverse relationship – that is, from the attachment figure to the child – and, as with attachment behaviour, it is possible to observe different kinds of caregiving behaviour. More sensitive and available carers (those to whom the child is more likely to be securely attached) tend to behave in more responsive ways to the child's needs. Such carers also incline towards making reasonably good predictions of what their child is thinking and feeling and what might be causing them distress or anxiety. Less sensitive and less physically or emotionally available carers (i.e. those to whom the child is more likely to have an insecure attachment relationship) tend to behave in less responsive ways. They may also experience more difficulty understanding what their child is thinking and feeling and may respond based on what they, the carers, is feeling instead; or their response might be based on how they would 'prefer' the child to be feeling.

Attachment theory has also been applied to adults, with many of the concepts relevant to children also having relevance for various adult relationships too. Clearly, the expression of these relationships is different for adults and in particular the expression of attachment behaviour will be significantly different for an adult than for a child. For example, a child may signal their attachment need by crying, raising their arms and vocalizing (but not necessarily verbalizing) that they want their attachment figure to give them a cuddle. Adults, on the other hand, tend not to express their attachment needs in quite the same way and may use far more complex and nuanced behaviour (although not always – it may be nothing more 'complex' than simply one adult coming home after work and immediately asking their partner for a hug). In conclusion, attachment theory is concerned with the universal human need for 'felt' security within attachment relationships and with the different ways in which security can be obtained and provided. Thus, whilst relationships are more diverse and in many ways more complicated than being 'only' about attachment, nevertheless, attachment relationships and behaviour are thought to be amongst the most important aspects of human relational experience. Hence an understanding of attachment theory is important for anyone whose professional practice leads them to work with people and with relationships.

'how to' guide

As previously noted, we have deliberately written this book for readers to engage with in different ways, to suit their own learning needs and the individual requirements of their interests and specialisms. However, we also appreciate that many readers will benefit from some guidance as to how they might read through the sections. To repeat what we have said already, we do not recommend reading the book from cover to cover, from A to Z, although that is certainly one possibility. Rather, we would suggest using the book in one of two ways.

Firstly, we suggest that many readers will find the book useful as a quick reference guide. Readers who use the book in this way may already be familiar with attachment theory but may either need some help and guidance with some of its more contemporary aspects, or they may be working in fields where although some reference is made to attachment theory it does not form part of the dominant theoretical discourse or body of knowledge. The following scenarios may help to illustrate what we mean:

- A child care lawyer in the process of reviewing social work assessments and reports in preparation for care proceedings might read a number of terms and, despite some degree of familiarity with attachment theory, may benefit from some further information. For example, a social worker may have written that the child's father lacks 'attunement' with the child and as a result, the social worker is concerned that the child may have an 'insecure attachment relationship' with him. The social worker may also note that at times, the father can be verbally aggressive towards the child and so the social worker is worried that the child may display 'disorganized attachment behaviour' (such a simplistic connection would need to be challenged and the references in this book will assist).
- A key worker in a residential home preparing for a meeting with a visiting psychologist to discuss the behaviour of one or two of the young people may benefit from a quick refresh of their knowledge with regards to some key concepts from attachment theory, such as the 'secure base' and 'internal working models'.
- A member of staff working with a new resident in a home for older people might be finding it difficult to understand some of his behaviour. They may note how his behaviour changes before and after visits from his life partner and (adult) children. The care worker may be familiar with attachment theory as it relates to children but feel less familiar with how it can illuminate experiences of separation, loss and bereavement in later life.

In these examples, one can see how this book might prove to be useful, potentially more so than a traditional textbook on attachment theory in which many references to various concepts are spread across a number of different chapters.

Second, the reader may want to use the book not (only) as a quick reference guide but as a way of exploring particular aspects of attachment theory in a more coherent way. For these readers, whilst it is entirely possible to 'jump in' and start reading (using the cross-referencing to help navigate around), we have also provided a number of 'recommended reading' guides, in the form of 'key themes'. Therefore, for each thematic heading we have selected a number of sections that we feel the reader will find useful, although of course it may still be helpful to follow the cross-referencing in any or all of these sections in order to further explore any areas of particular interest.

Attachment research (history and methods)	Attachment and children
• Adult Attachment Interview • Bowlby • Child Attachment Interview • Crittenden's Dynamic-Maturational Model (DMM) • criticisms of attachment theory • cultural differences • evolutionary insights • genetic influences • Harlow's monkey experiments • history of attachment theory and research • measures of attachment • memory • nature and nurture arguments • object relations theory • research methods in attachment • self-report measures of attachment • Story Stem Completion • Strange Situation Procedure • theory of mind • trans-generational transmission	• Child Attachment Interview • child maltreatment • disability • disorganized attachment • exploration and security • fathers • goal-oriented behaviour • internal working models • mothers • multiple attachments • neglected children • parenting • proximity-seeking and safe-haven behaviours • risk and resilience factors • secure attachment • secure base • separation protest • trans-generational transmission

Attachment difficulties	Assessing attachment
• (reactive) attachment disorder • disorganized attachment • dissociation • psychopathology and mental ill health • resilience and protective factors • unresolved loss and trauma	• Adult Attachment Interview • Child Attachment Interview • measures of attachment • self-report measures of attachment • Story Stem Completion • Strange Situation Procedure
Attachment and adults	**Caregiving**
• adult attachment • Adult Attachment Interview • attachment relationships in adulthood • ambivalent-resistant attachment • avoidant attachment • 'earned' (or 'acquired') security • insecure attachment • internal working models • later life attachments • loss and bereavement • romantic attachments • secure attachment	• attunement and sensitivity • bonding • cultural differences • emotion or 'affect' regulation • exploration and security • fathers • fostering and adoption • kinship care • mentalization and reflective function • mothers • multiple attachments • parenting • secure base
The use of attachment theory in policy and practice	**Attachment patterns and behaviour**
• criticisms of attachment theory • interventions • misuses of attachment theory • Video-based Intervention to Promote Positive Parenting	• ambivalent-resistant attachment • avoidant attachment • disorganized attachment • insecure attachment • secure attachment
Influences on attachment	
• attunement and sensitivity • child maltreatment • cultural differences • disability • gender • genetic influences • loss and bereavement • nature and nurture arguments	• neglected children • parenting • temperament • theory of mind • trans-generational transmission • unresolved loss and trauma • zero empathy

using attachment theory in practice

In the section on *interventions*, we discuss a number of notable applications of attachment theory to practice. However, in this final section of the introduction, we want to discuss in more general terms what we see as some of the problems in the way attachment theory has been applied to practice, particularly in the field of social care and social work. Typically, in our experience, most child and family social workers – indeed, most social workers of any variety – have at the very least a basic familiarity with attachment theory and with some of the key concepts such as secure and insecure attachment. Many health and social care professionals will also be aware of the correlation between secure attachment and a range of other positive outcomes for children and between insecure attachment – and particularly disorganized attachment behaviour – and a range of other, less positive outcomes. In some cases, we have seen some very informed and developed applications of attachment theory in practice, such as when social workers ask parents to 'speak for their child' as a way of assessing (and supporting) the parent's ability to mentalize. However, we have also seen what can only be described as quite crude and, in all likelihood, mistaken applications of attachment theory in practice. For example, we have read reports by contact supervisors observing that a child stays very physically close to their attachment figure throughout the session, with this then interpreted as a sign of 'positive attachment'; we see conclusions being drawn about a child's attachment relationships based on one, short observation; descriptions of parents being 'attached' to their babies; of a child's attachment relationship with their father being almost completely overlooked and of social workers describing young children as 'always happy and content' without reflecting on whether this is a 'good thing' or not. Additionally, we often hear workers speak of 'strong' attachments ... but markedly insecure attachments are often 'strong'; or 'good' attachments, when the worker presumably means 'secure' (and even more worryingly when they have not been in a position to assess this accurately).

Such examples – which we are sure will be familiar to many readers, if not necessarily from their own practice – have led us to conclude that applying attachment theory in practice should mean more than simply using it as a 'framework', in an imprecise sense.

Instead we believe attachment theory and research should only be applied using evidence-based techniques and methods of working, developed specifically for use in practice and with a particular client group (such as foster carers or the parents of abused or neglected children). In other words, whilst there can be great value in using attachment-related concepts as 'thinking tools' (e.g. to consider a young child's behaviour in respect of their attachment figure's potential as a secure base), there is more value in applying an actual technique to understand how the child is (or is not) actually able to use their attachment figure as a secure base. Of course, using these kinds of methods and tools in practice does require some expertise and specialized training. However, without the necessary investment of time and other resources that this requires, it seems that many well-meaning health and social care professionals are likely to go on misusing attachment theory in ways similar to those we briefly outlined earlier.

Finally, we have become increasingly worried that attachment theory and research are often used 'against' families: to highlight 'problems' or 'gaps' in parenting or caregiving relationships – particularly when writing reports for the courts or in relation to child protection procedures. Not only does this approach contradict the values that many health and social care professionals share in relation to the provision of effective help, challenging personal and social inequalities and working in partnership with families, it also overlooks the increasingly rich seam of studies that contribute to our understanding of how one can use insights from attachment theory to support families and their children. Thus, if you only remember one thing from this modest book (and we hope you might remember a little bit more than that), it would be this – attachment theory does not answer the question of what one 'should' do when working with families, nor does it dictate how children 'should' be cared for (other than perhaps in very broad terms) but used in the right way, it can assist you in providing the best, most effective help and support.

reference

Wilkins, D. (2014) 'The Use of Theory and Research Knowledge in Child Protection Social Work Practice: A Study of Disorganised Attachment and Child Protection Assessment', Unpublished PhD thesis (UK: University of Kent)

adult attachment

SEE ALSO Adult Attachment Interview; attachment relationships in adulthood; later life attachments; romantic attachments

Although attachment theory is more commonly discussed with regards to child–adult relationships, from the outset of his work *Bowlby* recognized that attachment could be a useful framework for understanding close human relationships from 'the cradle to the grave'. However, it was not until the 1980s that attachment researchers really began to focus on adult-to-adult relationships. As with any discussion of attachment, it is important to be clear on the distinction between an attachment and other kinds of *bonding* and of the key differences between adult-to-adult attachments and child-to-adult attachments. With regards to the former, an attachment is a specific type of bond, but attachment is not a synonym for bond or for relationship. For example, an adult may have a bond of friendship with another adult but may not have an attachment relationship to that friend. Equally, an elderly adult may have an attachment relationship with their adult child, without having a friendship bond with them. Put simply, in adulthood an attachment relationship is predicated on the reciprocated bond of caregiving, so that one might form an attachment relationship with a person providing significant and individualized levels of care. This also highlights one of the key differences between adult-to-adult attachment relationships when compared with child-to-adult attachment relationships, namely that for two adults, attachment and caregiving may operate in a bi-directional fashion. Thus, both adults may provide care for one another and be attached to one another at the same time. For younger children, they will not usually provide care for their adult attachment figures and so the attachment relationship is far more likely to be uni-directional, from child to adult, with the caregiving bond being uni-directional in reverse, from adult to child.

Returning to the development of attachment research concerning adults in the 1980s, Hazan and Shaver (1987) were amongst the first to study the concept with any degree of specificity and they began by noting the many similarities between attachment relationships in childhood and in adulthood. For example, many adults feel safer when their romantic partner is nearby or otherwise available for them, they may engage in regular close physical contact, they may feel insecure when their partner is inaccessible to them and they may express mutual fascination with each other. Any and all of these items could be applied to many child–adult relationships as well and, because of these similarities, Hazan and Shaver concluded that many (if not all) adult romantic relationships were also attachment relationships. This conceptualization of adult romantic relationships as potentially being attachment relationships (in addition to serving other 'functions' as well) leads to three possible implications. Firstly, if adult romantic relationships are attachment relationships, then we might expect to see differences in the nature and quality of these relationships in a similar way to the differences between certain infant attachment relationships (particularly in the categorization of these relationships as representing *secure attachment* or *insecure attachment*). Secondly, we may expect that the nature and quality of the attachment relationship will have implications for other aspects of adult behaviour, such as the willingness and confidence to explore (as in infants, individuals with secure attachment relationships might be expected to engage in more confident, exploratory behaviour). Thirdly, we might expect that an adult would bring his or her early experiences of attachment into any future romantic attachment relationships via their *internal working models* of attachment. However, this is not to assume that attachment patterns are fixed in childhood – they are not. Instead, an adult's attachment pattern is best understood as a reflection of their past experiences in combination with their current relational environment. Bartholomew (1990) considered how adult attachment could be represented by a two-dimensional construct of the adult's self-image and the adult's image of others (see Figure 1). From this perspective, it becomes possible to see how someone who developed a negative self-image in childhood but a positive image of others could, in their adult romantic relationships, develop a more positive self-image through the positive reinforcement of a partner

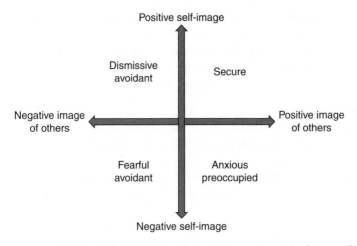

FIGURE 1   *Adult attachment patterns expressed as an interaction between the two dimensions of self-image and image of others*

(or partners) and come to develop a degree or *'earned' (or 'acquired') security*. This demonstrates one example of how internal working models may change and develop over time.

Research into the three questions posed by Hazan and Shaver (outlined earlier) has found the following. Using *self-report measures of attachment*, the distribution of adult attachment categories is similar to the distribution of infant attachment, with around 60 per cent secure, 20 per cent avoidant (dismissive or fearful) and 20 per cent anxious-resistant. From a meta-analysis of more than 10,000 *Adult Attachment Interviews* (AAIs), Bakermans-Kranenburg and van IJzendoorn (2009) found similar distributions, which is all the more interesting when one considers that the Adult Attachment Interview is a very different measure to self-report measures, with the former designed to access the adult's internal working models of attachment, whereas the latter accesses only self-reported attachment processes. There is also some evidence to suggest that many adults may seek out longer-term partners (probably unconsciously) who reinforce their expectations of attachment relationships. That is, adults with childhood experiences of *avoidant attachment* relationships may feel more comfortable in a romantic relationship with someone who does not attempt to get 'too close' to them or who overtly depends on them 'too much'. Alternatively, adults with childhood experiences of *ambivalent-resistant attachment* may find that a relationship with an adult who had avoidant childhood experiences feels 'too distant' or 'too remote' for them to really believe their partner genuinely loves and cares about them.

KEY TEXTS

- Benoit, D. and Parker, K. (1994) 'Stability and Transmission of Attachment Across Three Generations', *Child Development*, 65 (5): pp. 1444–1456
- Bifulco, A. and Thomas, G. (2012) *Understanding Adult Attachment in Family Relationships: Research, Assessment and Intervention* (London: Routledge)
- Hazan, C. and Shaver, P. (1987) 'Romantic Love Conceptualized as an Attachment Process', *Journal of Personality and Social Psychology*, 52 (3): pp. 511–524

Adult Attachment Interview

SEE ALSO **attachment relationships in adulthood; Child Attachment Interview**

The Adult Attachment Interview (AAI) is a way of understanding an adult's 'state of mind' with regards to attachment. Developed by George, Kaplan and Main in 1984, the AAI comprises 20 questions and usually takes about an hour to complete (see George, Kaplan and Main, 1996). The AAI aims to 'tap into' how the adult perceives his or her past attachment relationships and how they appraise the effects of these relationships on their development and current functioning. The aim of many of the questions is to access the adult's *memory* in relation to their early childhood experiences and particularly of the adult's childhood relationships with their attachment figures. However, the aim is not to test whether the adult can recall memories from their childhood or the specific nature of these memories but on how they have been 'processed' and on the coherence of the adult's account of them. For example, the third question of the AAI is:

I'd like to ask you to choose five adjectives or words that reflect your relationship with your mother starting from as far back as you can remember in early childhood … then I'd like to ask you why you chose them. (Main, 1996)

The exploration of 'why you chose them' is achieved by asking the person to recall particular examples or specific memories in relation to the words or phrases chosen. The tenth question is:

> In general, how do you think your overall experiences with your parents have affected your adult personality? (ibid.)

At this point, it is important to note the difference between an attachment pattern and an attachment state of mind. The former refers to the nature of a child's attachment behaviour towards an attachment figure (and can be categorized as *ambivalent-resistant attachment, avoidant attachment, disorganized attachment* or *secure attachment*). The latter refers to the notion that, by adulthood, a child's individual attachments to their childhood attachment figures will have coalesced into a particular – and classifiable – state of mind with regards to attachment. This hypothesis, which has been demonstrated empirically (Furman and Simon, 2004), suggests that childhood attachment-related experiences will tend towards integrated and coherent *internal working models* as the child grows older and certainly by the time they reach adulthood (but see *genetic influences*).

As with the *Strange Situation Procedure*, the AAI needs to be completed and analysed by a trained coder in order that the adult can be assigned a formal attachment classification. For example, the responses of participants are analysed with regards to their internal coherence and in relation to Grice's (1975) maxims of 'be truthful' (does the respondent provide examples in support of what they are saying?), 'be concise' (does the respondent provide sufficient information in order to answer the question or do they say too much or too little for the interviewer to understand what they actually mean?), 'be relevant' (does the respondent provide mostly relevant information or are they prone to providing tangential information?) and 'be clear' (is it clear to the interviewer what the respondent is saying or is the respondent prone to ambiguity and obscurity?).

As noted earlier, AAI classifications were, at least initially, based on the Ainsworth infant attachment patterns of secure attachment, ambivalent-resistant attachment and avoidant attachment, albeit with amended terminology to reflect the application to adults – secure-autonomous (associated with the infant secure classification), dismissing (associated with the infant avoidant classification) and preoccupied (associated with the infant ambivalent-resistant classification (see Box 1). The concept of *'earned' (or 'acquired') security* was later devised in order to account for adults who seemed to describe *insecure attachment* relationships in childhood but who presented contemporaneously with secure-autonomous states of mind (and it is also important to note that a minority of adults cannot be classified at all via the AAI).

One particularly interesting aspect of these early studies using the AAI was that often they involved the same adults who had previously been studied along with their children using the Strange Situation Procedure. In these earlier studies, it was the children who were being studied and assigned an attachment classification. Having completed studies using both the AAI and the Strange Situation Procedure, involving the same child–adult dyads, the researchers found that where the child was categorized as having a secure attachment relationship, their attachment figure was most likely to be categorized as having a secure-autonomous state of mind. Equally, if the child had been categorized as having an avoidant attachment or ambivalent-resistant attachment relationship, the attachment figure was most likely to be categorized as having a dismissing or preoccupied state of mind respectively. What this demonstrated was the possibility of being able to predict the nature of the child's attachment relationship to a particular attachment figure based on an analysis of the attachment figure's state of mind with regards to attachment and vice versa. Remarkably, this remained the case even when the researchers analysed maternal states of mind prior to the birth of the child (see Benoit and Parker, 1994) although it is important to consider the possibility of genetic influences as well as environmental influences, with the relationship between the two being more complex and intriguing than initially understood.

Several years after the initial development of the AAI, a fourth category of 'unresolved' was developed and this category seemed to be linked to disorganized attachment behaviour in the child. Just as disorganized attachment behaviour may be thought of as representing a 'breakdown' in the child's organized attachment behaviour, so the 'unresolved' category for adults may be seen as representing a 'breakdown' in the adult's ability to provide a coherent narrative (although it is important to note that neither of these represents an actual psychological or psychiatric disorder). For the child, their behaviour may 'breakdown' when they cannot resolve the twin goals of seeking comfort from an attachment figure and of moving away from or otherwise protecting themselves from the same attachment figure. Similarly in the AAI this 'breakdown' can be seen in the inability of the adult to answer the questions in a coherent way, most commonly seen when the questions relate to memories of loss or abuse. This may occur particularly when the adult is asked about situations of *unresolved loss and trauma*.

When an AAI interview is analysed, trained coders consider not just 'what' the adults says in their answers but 'the ways' in which they say it. One aspect of this analysis is to consider whether the adult is able to provide evidence for what they say. For example, if they said that their father was always caring, are they able to give some examples of when their father behaved in a caring way? The coder would also be interested in whether the adult was giving succinct answers, whether they were able to answer the questions without providing a lot of irrelevant information and whether they were able to remain coherent during the interview. The coder would also be interested in whether the adult was able to focus on different aspects of the questions. For example, can they talk about their memories of childhood and reflect on what those memories mean to them without becoming either confused or fixated with just the memories or just what they mean to them? Adults with secure-autonomous states of mind tend to be able to shift their focus quite easily between the memories themselves and the meaning of those memories whereas, for example, adults with dismissing states of mind will tend to avoid talking about attachment-related memories and adults with preoccupied states of mind will tend to get 'caught up' in their memories at the expense of coherence (Main, 2000). Using the AAI, most adults are classified as having a secure-autonomous state of mind and this remains the case regardless of where the adults are from, their background or culture or what language the interview is completed in. It is only when the AAI is used with adults in 'at risk' groups that significantly different outcomes are seen. For example, if the adult has a psychiatric disorder they are more likely to be classified as having an insecure state of mind or as 'cannot classify' (Bakermans-Kranenburg and van IJzendoorn, 2009).

7

An alternative approach to the analysis of the AAI as outlined above exists in the form of *Crittenden's Dynamic-Maturational Model* (DMM). Using Crittenden's model will tend to produce different classifications as this approach has greater complexity in terms of attachment categories and sub-categories. Conceptually, the DMM focuses more on how adults seek to protect themselves from discomfort or threats in the present than on how they might have been cared for in the past.

KEY TEXTS

- Bakermans-Kranenburg, M. and van IJzendoorn, M. (2009) 'The First 10,000 Adult Attachment Interviews: Distributions of Adult Attachment Representations in Clinical and Non-clinical Groups', *Attachment and Human Development*, 11 (3): pp. 223–263
- George, C., Kaplan, N. and Main, M. (1996) *Adult Attachment Interview Protocol*. 3rd edn. Unpublished Manuscript (Berkeley: University of California). Available at http://www.psychology.sunysb.edu/attachment/measures/content/aai_interview.pdf
- Hesse, E. (2008) 'The Adult Attachment Interview' in J. Cassidy and P. Shaver (eds), *Handbook of Attachment, Theory, Research and Clinical Applications*. 2nd edn (New York, NY: Guilford Press), pp. 552–598

BOX 1: *Some example responses to the Adult Attachment Interview*

Interviewer: The first word you have to describe your relationship with your mother during childhood was 'loving'. Can you think of a memory or incident that would illustrate for me why you chose that word?

Respondent: I don't remember ... (5 second pause). Well, because she was caring and supportive.

Interviewer: Well, this can be difficult because a lot of people haven't thought about these things for a long time, but take a minute and see if you can think of an incident or example.

Respondent: (10 second pause) Well ... (5 second pause) I guess like, well, you know, she was really pretty and she took a lot of care with her appearance. Whenever she drove me to school, I was always really proud of that when we pulled up at the playground.

Note that the participant does not answer the question. At first, s/he simply provides further descriptive words (caring and supportive). Then, s/he gives a positive description of the mother but again, does not give an example of when she was 'loving' as initially requested by the interviewer. If this pattern continued throughout the interview, it would likely be classified as dismissing.

Respondent: Loving… (5 second pause). I don't know if this is the sort of thing you are looking for, but one thing that comes to mind is the way she stuck up for me if I got in trouble at school… I just knew where I stood with her, and that she'd be comforting if I was upset or crying or something.

Interviewer: Thank you (interrupted).

Respondent: Oh you wanted a specific example. Um, that time I set fire to the garage… expected to get the life lectured out of me, but she just ran straight for me and picked me up and hugged me real hard. Guess she was so scared and so glad to see me… that was very loving.

Source: Extracts taken from Hesse (2008, p. 558).

Note the clear example of a specific time when the mother was 'loving' and the way the participant concludes at the end by linking back to the question asked. If this pattern continued throughout the interview, it would likely be classified as secure-autonomous.

ambivalent-resistant attachment

SEE ALSO avoidant attachment; disorganized attachment; secure attachment

To what extent would you tend to agree or disagree with the following statements?

- I find that others are reluctant to get as close as I would like.
- I often worry my partner doesn't really love me or want to stay with me.
- I want to merge completely with another person and this desire sometimes scares people away.

9

If you agreed with these statements (see *self-report measures of attachment*), you may have a 'preoccupied' state of mind with regards to attachment. According to several large-scale and cross-cultural studies of typical populations, around 19 per cent of adults have a preoccupied state of mind (Bakermans-Kranenburg and van IJzendoorn, 2009) and around 10 per cent of children have an ambivalent-resistant attachment relationship (van IJzendoorn and Kroonenberg, 1988). There are some *cultural differences* in these distributions between different populations but for the most part, these are not particularly significant in the majority of cases.

As with the categories of *avoidant attachment* and *secure attachment*, the category of ambivalent-resistant was first discovered in relation to infants via the use of the *Strange Situation Procedure*. When Mary Ainsworth and her colleagues devised the Strange Situation Procedure, they predicted that infants would behave differently towards their attachment figures on separation and subsequent reunion and that infants would also behave differently in terms of how they explored the room and played with the toys. What they did not predict was that it would be possible to categorize the majority of infants into just three categories of attachment pattern – avoidant attachment, ambivalent-resistant attachment and secure attachment. As with the *Adult Attachment Interview*, Ainsworth and others also found that a number of infants could not be categorized at all using these three patterns and it was from subsequent study of this group of children that the concept of *disorganized attachment* behaviour would arise.

Were you to observe an infant in the Strange Situation Procedure, one who had an ambivalent-attachment relationship with their primary carer, you would see two types of behaviour in particular – a relatively intense level of distress upon separation from their attachment figure and an apparent inability to accept any comfort offered by the attachment figure upon reunion. Such infants may quickly approach their attachment figure when they return, vocalizing their distress and 'obviously' seeking comfort. Many times, their attachment figure will offer them comfort and although the infant may seem to initially accept this comfort, they will nevertheless continue to express their distress. They may ask to be picked up and cuddled but then when put back down again, quickly become distressed again. In more extreme examples, the infant may demonstrate a desire to be picked up but then push the attachment figure away when they attempt to do so. After the first episode of separation, these infants tend to pay less attention to the toys than they did before, seemingly remaining vigilant for any signs that the attachment figure might leave again.

Bowlby and Ainsworth theorized that all children develop *internal working models* of attachment. In the case of children with ambivalent-resistant attachment relationships, this model essentially says 'exaggerate the distress you feel and the need you have for your attachment figure as this is the most effective way of ensuring that you receive some form of comfort. If you display lower levels of distress, you will not necessarily receive any attention'. When studying the behaviour of the attachment figures of infants with ambivalent-resistant attachment relationships, it becomes clear that they tend to offer comfort inconsistently. At times, they may reject displays of distress by the infant whilst at other times appearing to be quite sensitive. It is this lack of consistency that is thought to cause the infant to exaggerate their distress, to increase the likelihood that the attachment figure will respond, and thus the infant's behaviour can be understood as *goal-oriented behaviour*. As infants grow and develop into middle childhood, they tend to become less distressed by the kind of short separation episodes used in the Strange Situation Procedure and by the age of 4, *separation protest* has usually diminished significantly. By age 7–11, children tend to be more concerned with the psychological and emotional availability of their attachment figures than their actual physical proximity. Thus, the Strange Situation Procedure is no longer a viable method of measuring attachment and so other attachment measures are used such as *Story Stem Completion*.

With regards to *adult attachment*, it is more common to refer to 'preoccupied' states of mind than ambivalent-resistant attachment. Adults with a preoccupied state of mind will identify the importance of close relationships and feel strongly dependent on others. However, they will also worry that other people do not really value them or care about them and so may develop a negative view of self. It is important to remember that neither the attachment pattern nor the state of mind is considered pathological; indeed, some argue that all attachment behaviour is adaptive to a particular caregiving environment and therefore it is wrong to conceptualize any one pattern or state of mind as being any 'worse' or 'more optimal' than any other – an approach that is most explicit in *Crittenden's Dynamic-Maturational Model* (DMM).

KEY TEXTS
- Cassidy, J. and Berlin, L. (1994) 'The Insecure/Ambivalent Pattern of Attachment: Theory and Research', *Child Development*, 65 (4): pp. 971–991
- McCarthy, G. and Taylor, A. (1999) 'Avoidant/Ambivalent Attachment Style as a Mediator between Abusive Childhood Experiences and Adult Relationship Difficulties', *Journal of Child Psychology and Psychiatry*, 40 (3): pp. 465–477
- Scher, A. and Mayseless, O. (2000) 'Mothers of Anxious/Ambivalent Infants: Maternal Characteristics and Child-Care Context', *Child Development*, 71 (6): pp. 1629–1639

(reactive) attachment disorder

SEE ALSO **child maltreatment; disorganized attachment; neglected children; psychopathology and mental ill health**

Reactive Attachment disorder is a broad term, referring to problematic moods, behaviours and relationships thought to arise from an early failure to form 'normal' attachments. However, and as noted by Prior and Glaser (2006), there are two discourses with regards to attachment disorder. The first is grounded in a scientific, psychiatric discipline, based on careful study, diagnosis and treatment. The second is based largely on unfounded (non-scientific) claims, often with no basis in attachment theory. Unfortunately, much of the information about this second discourse is readily available on the Internet and thus, for the curious practitioner, it is relatively easy to be misled. In contrast, much of the information in relation to the first discourse is essentially hidden within academic journals (often behind expensive pay walls) and this makes it difficult for busy health and social care workers (often working in resource-poor organizations) to access. As an example of the former, one can easily find 'symptom checklists' for attachment disorder, which often include items such as:

- cruelty towards animals;
- victimizes others (bullies);

- lack of eye contact;
- preoccupation with fire, gore or evil;
- lack of remorse or conscience;
- making false allegations (of abuse), lying about the 'obviously true' (crazy lying).

The problem with these kinds of checklists is twofold – firstly, they have little or no relation to formal methods for identifying attachment disorders and secondly, many of the items included have little or no relation to attachment at all (e.g. a preoccupation with fire, gore or evil). In practice, some of the items may even be dangerous – for example, if 'false allegations of abuse' are taken to be indicative of an attachment disorder and the child is labelled as having an attachment disorder, how might this influence perceptions of any future allegations the child might make? For the sake of absolute clarity, we see no justification for the use of these kinds of checklists within health and social care practice.

On the other hand, the criteria for attachment disorder included within the World Health Organization's International Classification of Diseases does have scientific validity although there is an ongoing debate, of course, about the exact nature and features of attachment disorders, on how widely such diagnostic criteria should be used and so on – most importantly, these criteria must be administered by suitably trained and experienced clinicians.

As an example of a valid application of the concept of attachment disorder in practice with children, Chisholm (1998) studied the development of a group of Romanian children who spent much of their early lives living in orphanages in deplorable conditions and who subsequently were adopted. As described by Chisholm, many of these children were exposed to caregiving environments in which they were unable to develop attachment relationships but, once adopted, many of them were able to form attachments with their new carers although they also continued to demonstrate indiscriminately friendly behaviour towards strangers. This behaviour was observed not just in the immediate period after they were adopted but some years later as well. In other words, even though many of these children went on to form normal attachment relationships with their adoptive carers, some elements of their previous experiences seemed to persist. Nevertheless, even when a child may have experienced very deprived and neglectful caregiving, it is important to be open-minded about whether an attachment disorder is the best conception of any presenting difficulties and to use holistic assessments of the child's needs, rather than focusing solely on particular diagnostic criteria alone (Woolgar and Scott, 2013).

KEY TEXTS

- Chisholm, K. (1998) 'A Three-Year Follow-Up of Attachment and Indiscriminate Friendliness in Children Adopted from Romanian Orphanages', *Child Development*, 69 (4): pp. 1092–1106
- Prior, V. and Glaser, D. (2006) *Understanding Attachment and Attachment Disorders: Theory, Evidence and Practice* (London: Jessica Kingsley)
- Shemmings, D. (2014) 'Disorganised Attachment and Reactive Attachment Disorders' in P. Holmes and S. Farnfield (eds), *The Routledge Handbook of Attachment, Vol 1: Theory* (London: Routledge)
- Woolgar, M. and Scott, S. (2013) 'The Negative Consequences of Over-diagnosing Attachment Disorders in Adopted Children: The Importance of Comprehensive Formulations', *Clinical Child Psychology and Psychiatry*, 19 (3): pp. 355–366

attachment relationships in adulthood

SEE ALSO **adult attachment; Adult Attachment Interview; later life attachments; romantic attachments**

The study of attachment relationships in adulthood is in many ways a natural progression from the initial focus within attachment theory on the attachment and caregiving relationships between infants and their attachment figures. This progression is predicated on the notion that the same – or similar – impulses and systems that guide the attachment and caregiving bonds between infants and their attachment figures are also responsible for at least a part of the close attachment relationships that develop between some adults. However, although the *history of attachment theory and research* clearly shows research regarding *adult attachment* developing later than research regarding child attachment, *Bowlby* was clear from the outset of his work that he believed attachment characterizes human relational experiences from 'the cradle to the grave'. Hazan and Shaver (1987) were amongst the first researchers to apply attachment theory to adult-to-adult relationships and although they focused on *romantic attachments*, this does not preclude an understanding of attachment as applied to other kinds of adult relationships as well. Hazan and Shaver noted that romantic attachments often share a number of features with infant attachment relationships, such as:

- a feeling of safety when the other is nearby;
- a feeling of relative insecurity when the other is inaccessible;
- engaging in close, physical, bodily contact;
- sharing one another's positive affect (such as pleasant surprise, happiness and joy) and negative effect (such as pain and upset).

However, although romantic relationships are significantly important for many adults, they are clearly not the only kind of close relationships that adults form. Many adults will continue to have close relationships with their own childhood attachment figures well into adulthood and this may involve at times something of a 'role-reversal' in later life, with the adult child providing care for the ageing attachment figure and this 'role-reversal' may play an important in *later life attachments*. Equally, many adults form very close but non-romantic relationships with other adults based on friendship. Therefore, it has been of some interest to attachment researchers as to how far (or not) attachment characterizes a number of different types of adult-to-adult relationships, in addition to romantic ones.

One question regarding the role of attachment in adult relationships is whether attachment remains a relationship-specific construct, as it is in childhood, or whether it becomes more akin to a characteristic of the individual. In Bowlby's original writings, he supposed that in the early years of life, attachment is relationship-specific (i.e. the child may have different types of attachment relationships with different attachment figures) but that over time, these different *internal working models* coalesce into a more coherent state of mind with regards to attachment. However, the evidence from the relatively few research studies that have explicitly addressed this question suggest that the relationship-specific construct remains valid for longer than early childhood and possibly even across the lifespan (but see *genetic influences*). For example, Imamoğlu and Imamoğlu (2006) found that in relation to attachment figures, friends and romantic partners, young adults reported differing levels of security based on experiences exclusive to a particular relationship. In a large study of 2,214 young adults, Caron *et al.* (2012) also found that patterns of attachment differ depending on the particular relationship being considered and this again supports the concept of attachment as a relationship-specific construct, at least in young adulthood. This same study also found that relationships between adults-as-friends and adults-as-romantic-partners tend to have more in common with each other than with the adult's childhood attachment relationships, perhaps something that can be explained by the 'voluntary' (if somewhat happenstance) nature of many friendships and romantic relationships, at least when compared with the unilateral relationship that most children have with their attachment figures (i.e. children have no or only very limited choice as to who cares for them when compared with adults).

Finally, although Hazan and Shaver identified several important ways in which adult-to-adult attachment relationships may be similar to child attachment relationships, there is also (at least) one key difference. Namely, that in child attachment relationships, the 'attachment' is from the child to the adult, with the 'caregiving' aspect of the relationship primarily operating in the reverse direction (i.e. from the adult to the child). In adult-to-adult relationships, it will often be the case that both individuals have an attachment relationship with each other, and at the same time they may also be one another's carer (although this is not to suggest that the balance will always be equally split all of the time – and why should it be? – nor that the nature of these bonds will be the same for both individuals).

KEY TEXTS

- Caron, A., Lafontaine, M., Bureau, J., Levesque, C. and Johnson, S. (2012) 'Comparisons of Close Relationships: An Evaluation of Relationship Quality and Patterns of Attachment to Parents, Friends, and Romantic Partners in Young Adults', *Canadian Journal of Behavioural Science*, 44 (4): pp. 245–256
- Crowell, J. and Treboux, D. (1995) 'A Review of Adult Attachment Measures: Implications for Theory and Research', *Social Development*, 4: pp. 294–327

- Hazan, R. and Shaver, P. (1987) 'Romantic Love Conceptualized as an Attachment Process', *Journal of Personality and Social Psychology*, 52 (3): pp. 511–524

attunement and sensitivity

SEE ALSO **emotion (or 'affect') regulation; mentalization and reflective function; theory of mind**

Attunement and sensitivity are key concepts in attachment theory. Indeed, Sroufe (1995) has conceptualized attachment, especially in the early years, as a process for *emotion (or 'affect') regulation*. This conception recognizes that infants are not capable of regulating their own emotions and therefore, they require the help of other people for two reasons: firstly, to regulate their emotions and secondly, to 'teach' them how to self-regulate. So, for example, if an attachment figure leaves the infant alone for a few minutes, such as may occur several times during the *Strange Situation Procedure*, most infants will become distressed and display some form of *separation protest*. Upon reunion, most attachment figures, and especially those with whom the infant has a secure attachment relationship, will attempt to soothe the child through physical contact but also by talking to the child and 'putting words' around their distress. The attachment figure might say things like 'you're upset aren't you but don't worry, daddy is back now' or 'it's okay to be upset when mummy leaves, but mummy's back now, okay?' By so doing, these attachment figures are demonstrating attunement, showing the child that not only have they noticed the infant's distress but that they also understand the (possible) reasons for it.

Thus, in the field of attachment theory and research, attunement refers to the attachment figure's capacity to sensitively read and understand the infant's signals, both verbal and non-verbal, and to put him or herself in the mind of the infant. Attunement in semantic terms has a rather poetic definition, meaning to 'bring into harmony with'. Note the difference between 'bring into harmony with' and 'being in harmony with', the former implying an active process, whereas the latter (potentially) implies a passive one. It is also possible to see how attachment figures who are more able to sensitively understand their infant's signals – and attune with them – are more likely to promote a well-developed capacity for self-regulation on the part of the infant as they grow older. Based on this assumption, it is unsurprising that attachment researchers have found a relatively strong correlation between attachment figures who demonstrate higher levels of sensitivity and attunement and children with *secure attachment* relationships (see Parker, 2010). Earlier studies also found that *mothers* with secure-autonomous states of mind with regards attachment were more able to attune with a wider range of emotional states whereas mothers with dismissing states of mind tended not to attune with negative emotional states (such as distress), although they did attune with more positive emotional states (such as happiness). On the other hand, mothers with preoccupied states of mind were seen to inconsistently attune to both positive and negative emotional states. It is important to note that although much of this research has been undertaken with mothers, we must be careful not to assume either that father's cannot or do not attune with their infants as well as mother's nor that maternal attunement is more important or more significant, necessarily, than paternal attunement.

There has also been some fascinating research regarding levels of attunement between children and their mothers on a physiological level in addition to the behavioural level. In a rather neat experiment, Sethre-Hofstad *et al.* (2002) challenged a number of children (aged between two and four years of age) to walk across a balance beam for the first time whilst their mothers watched on a monitor from another room. Prior to this task, the mothers were observed playing with their children and these interactions were coded for the levels of sensitivity shown by the mothers. Just before the beam task and at 30 minutes afterwards, saliva samples were collected from the children and the mothers and these samples were examined for the amount of cortisol they contained. Cortisol is a naturally occurring hormone within the body with many and various functions but one of its primary roles is the mediation of stress. In response to stressful situations, the body tends to release cortisol in order to activate a number of 'anti-stress' pathways (to return the body to a state of physiological homeostasis). Sethre-Hofstad *et al.* (2002) wondered whether there would be a relationship between the more sensitive mothers and the levels of cortisol in the child's and the mother's saliva, following the beam task. What they found was that mothers from the highly sensitive group had cortisol levels significantly correlated with the child's cortisol levels whereas mothers from the less sensitive group had levels of cortisol that were not significantly related to those of the child. What these data suggest is that – in a physical sense – more sensitive mothers (and unfortunately this experiment only included mothers) 'feel' what their child is feeling when under stress (or at least, they have a similar physical reaction to the child). As the child became more stressed by the challenge of walking across a balance beam and as their bodies released the cortisol hormone in response, so the more sensitive mothers seemed to feel an increased level of stress as well, and to a remarkably similar degree to their child. In summary, security of attachment in childhood is correlated with increased levels of sensitivity and attunement by the attachment figure. Not only do sensitive attachment figures respond in a behaviourally attuned way to their child, they may also respond in similar physiological ways.

Attunement and sensitivity are also important concepts for *adult attachment*. In particular, research by McCluskey, Hooper and Miller (1999) in this area suggests that one of the key factors determining whether or not an adult 'feels helped' by a professional is the degree to which they experience an empathic attunement with them. McCluskey and colleagues highlighted how this process may be similar to that observed in relation to infants, of care-seeking and care-giving, and of the need to ensure a degree of synchronicity between these two 'systems' of behaviour. This research may help us to understand why it is that some adults, even when apparently in need of help, find it more difficult to seek and to accept help. For example, if the adult has a history of being rejected or dismissed when in need of help, such that they had *avoidant attachment* relationships with their childhood attachment figures, they may want to downplay their need for any help or they may employ strategies that have proven successful in the past. For example, they may attempt to provide care rather than receive it or they may try to 'dominate' the professional who is attempting to help them.

KEY TEXTS

- McCluskey, U., Hooper, C. A. and Miller, L. (1999) 'Goal-Corrected Empathic Attunement: Developing and Rating the Concept within

an Attachment Perspective', *Psychotherapy: Theory, Research, Practice, Training*, 36 (1): pp. 80–90
- Meins, E. (2013) 'Sensitive Attunement to Infants' Internal States: Operationalizing the Construct of Mind-Mindedness', *Attachment and Human Development*, 15 (5–6): pp. 524–544
- Sroufe, L. A. (1995) *Emotional Development: The Organization of Emotional Life in the Early Years* (New York: Cambridge University Press)

avoidant attachment

SEE ALSO **ambivalent-resistant attachment; disorganized attachment; secure attachment**

To what extent would you tend to agree or disagree with the following statements?

- I am comfortable without close emotional relationships.
- It is very important to me to feel independent and self-sufficient.
- I prefer not to depend on others or have others depend on me.

If you agreed with these statements (see *self-report measures of attachment*), you may have a 'dismissing' state of mind with regards to attachment. According to several large-scale and cross-cultural studies of typical populations, around 23 per cent of adults have a dismissing state of mind (Bakermans-Kranenburg and van IJzendoorn, 2009) and around 20 per cent of children have an *avoidant attachment* relationship (van IJzendoorn and Kroonenberg, 1988). There are some *cultural differences* in these distributions between different populations but, for the most part, these are not particularly significant in the majority of cases.

As with the categories of *ambivalent-resistant attachment* and *secure attachment*, the category of avoidant attachment was first discovered in relation to infants via the use of the *Strange Situation Procedure*. When Mary Ainsworth and her colleagues devised the Strange Situation Procedure, they predicted that infants would behave differently towards their attachment figures on separation and following reunion and that the infants would also behave differently in terms of how they explored the room and played with the toys. What they did not predict was that it would be possible to categorize the majority of infants into just three categories of attachment pattern – avoidant attachment, ambivalent-resistant attachment and secure attachment. As with the *Adult Attachment Interview*, Ainsworth and others also found that a number of infants could not be categorized at all using these three patterns and it was from subsequent study of this group of children that the concept of *disorganized attachment* behaviour would arise.

Were you to observe an infant in the Strange Situation Procedure, one who had an avoidant attachment relationship with their primary carer, you would see three types of behaviour in particular – more limited exploration, a more limited degree of *separation protest* as the attachment figure leaves, and a more subdued response when the attachment figure returns. However, this is not to say that infants with avoidant attachment relationships are less distressed by separation from their attachment figures, only that they have learned to inhibit their outward display of this distress. When such infants are monitored for physiological signs of distress during the Strange Situation Procedure, it becomes clear that although they may not outwardly display distress, physiologically they are distressed as shown by increased palpitation and perspiration. These changes are suggestive of levels of distress similar to – if not more so than – children with secure attachment relationships. Upon reunion, infants with avoidant attachment relationships tend to return to exploring the room or playing with the toys but with a less focused engagement than infants with secure attachments and hence, their return to play is best understood as a 'displacement activity', an attempt to avoid (further) rejection by the attachment figure.

Bowlby and Ainsworth theorized that all children develop *internal working models* of attachment and in the case of children with avoidant attachment relationships, this model essentially says 'do not demonstrate that you need your attachment figure, this will cause them to reject you. The best way of obtaining or maintaining proximity to an attachment figure is to act as if you do not need them'. When studying the behaviour of the attachment figures of infants with avoidant attachment relationships, it becomes clear that they tend to reliably reject external displays of distress, they tend to be less emotionally expressive and they tend to have a greater aversion to physical contact. Studies outside of the Strange Situation Procedure have confirmed the presence of similar behaviours in the

21

home environment as well. Thus, the infant's behaviour – inhibiting their own external display of distress in order to reduce the chance of the attachment figure rejecting them – can be described as *goal-oriented behaviour*, with the goal being to maintain at least some level of proximity to the attachment figure. As infants grow and develop into middle childhood, they tend to become less distressed by the kind of short separation episodes used in the Strange Situation Procedure and by the age of 4, separation protest has usually diminished significantly. By age 7–11, children are more concerned with the psychological and emotional availability of their attachment figures than their actual physical proximity. Thus, the Strange Situation Procedure is no longer a viable method of measuring attachment and so other attachment measures are used such as *Story Stem Completion* or the *Child Attachment Interview* (CAI).

With regards to *adult attachment*, it is more common to refer to 'dismissing' states of mind rather than avoidant attachment. Adults with a dismissing state of mind with regards to attachment will tend to identify the importance of feeling independent and may view close relationships as relatively unimportant. There is another form of adult avoidant attachment known as fearful-avoidant and adults with this state of mind will tend to agree with the following statements:

- I am somewhat uncomfortable getting close to others.
- I find it difficult to trust others completely or depend on them.
- I sometimes worry that I will be hurt if I allow myself to become too close to others.

Comparing these statements with those at the start of this section, we can see that the latter are more 'worrying' variations of the former. In addition, the latter set point to a concern about the possibility of being harmed by becoming close to another person. This suggests perhaps more extreme experiences of being rejected by an attachment figure. Nevertheless, it is important to bear in mind that neither the dismissing nor the fearful-avoidant states of mind are pathological; indeed, some argue that all attachment behaviour is adaptive to a particular caregiving environment and therefore it is wrong to conceptualize any one pattern or state of mind as being any 'worse' or 'more optimal' than any other – this approach is most explicit in *Crittenden's Dynamic-Maturational Model* (DMM).

KEY TEXTS

- Bartholomew, K. (1990) 'Avoidant of Intimacy: An Attachment Perspective', *Journal of Social and Personal Relationships*, 7 (2): pp. 147–178
- Rholes, S., Simpson, J. and Friedman, M. (2006) 'Avoidant Attachment and the Experience of Parenting', *Personality and Social Psychology Bulletin*, 32 (3): pp. 275–285
- Robert, M. (2009) Trauma and Dismissing (Avoidant) Attachment: Intervention Strategies in Individual Psychotherapy', *Psychotherapy: Theory, Research, Practice, Training*, 46 (1): pp. 68–81

b

bonding

SEE ALSO internal working models; proximity-seeking and safe-haven behaviours; secure base

In every day parlance, at least in the field of social care, it is quite common for the words 'bond' and 'attachment' to be used interchangeably, as in the following example:

This child and his mother share a strong bond.
This child and her mother share a strong attachment.

However, when discussing relationships within the context of attachment theory, the word 'attachment' is not a synonym for bond (or bonding). Bonding is a more general term, used with reference to many different kinds of relationship, whereas attachment is more specific, describing the use of another human being as a *secure base* and as the focus of *proximity-seeking and safe-haven behaviours* at times of heightened anxiety. Within attachment relationships, there is a sense of 'turning to someone else for safety' and for 'felt security'. Note how this would (in almost all circumstances) preclude an adult from being attached to their own child, certainly whilst the child were still relatively young (we would not go to a baby 'for' comfort and protection when we were frightened, rather we would go to the baby in order to 'provide' comfort and protection).

The reciprocal bond that an *adult attachment* figure (almost always) develops with their child is known in attachment theory as a caregiving bond. As the infant develops an attachment relationship with his or her primary carer, so the primary carer develops a caregiving bond with the infant. Prior and Glaser (2006, p. 57) argue that this caregiving bond 'involves a commitment to care for and protect the child and (an) intense emotion, which is typically experienced as love'. Thus, in most relationships between an infant and an adult attachment figure, both individuals develop a bond with one another but of a qualitatively different nature – one involves the provision of care (from the attachment figure to the infant or child) and one involves the expectation of care and protection (by the infant or child of the attachment figure). In terms of adult attachment, two or more adults may share an attachment relationship and a caregiving bond with one another at the same time.

Attachment relationships may also relate to other kinds of bonds via the influence of *internal working models*. As infants develop a sense of self and of what to expect from other people, partly as a result of their experiences of early attachment relationships, so they develop a set of implicit expectations and relational patterns of behaviour that they often take with them into other relationships.

KEY TEXTS
- Gao, Y., Raine, A., Chan, F., Venables, P. and Mednick, S. (2010) 'Early Maternal and Paternal Bonding, Childhood Physical Abuse and Adult Psychopathic Personality', *Psychological Medicine*, 40 (6): pp. 1007–1016
- Insel, T. and Young, L. (2001) The Neurobiology of Attachment', *Nature Reviews*, 2: pp. 129–136
- Redshaw, M. and Martin, C. (2013) 'Babies, "Bonding" and Ideas about Parental "Attachment"', *Journal of Reproductive and Infant Psychology*, doi: 10.1080/02646838.2013.830383

Bowlby

SEE ALSO **history of attachment theory and research; research methods in attachment**

Edward John Mostyn Bowlby (1907–1990) was the British psychiatrist who contributed most to the development of early attachment theory via his pioneering work in the field.

John Bowlby believed that infants needed more from their primary carers than the (relatively) simple provision of nourishment and warmth to meet their basic needs. In part, he found support for this belief in *Harlow's monkey experiments*, undertaken in the 1930s, which seemed to demonstrate that, at least in non-human primate species, young infants need to feel a sense of comfort and protection from their primary carers as much as they need for them to provide food – what Harlow called 'contact comfort'. Bowlby called this need for comfort and protection an 'attachment' relationship. Over time, Bowlby's insights transformed many aspects of child welfare policy and practice, including bringing to an end, for the most part, the use of residential nurseries for children, as well as other practices that involved the prolonged separation of children from their attachment figures (e.g. during hospital inpatient admissions).

In addition to Harlow's monkey experiments, Bowlby's early work was also influenced by the experience of many children during the Second World War of being separated from their primary carers. This included children evacuated from the major cities of Britain during the war, the movement of thousands of Jewish children to Britain in the months preceding the start of the war in 1939 (often without other family members), the policy of placing large numbers of children in group nurseries in order that their *mothers* could work and contribute to the national war effort and the experiences of orphaned children. After the Second World War, Bowlby also became interested in the reactions of children to much shorter or less permanent separations, such as those in hospital, and he was influenced in his thinking by the work of James Robertson, a social worker and psychoanalyst, to the extent that Bowlby would later write '(He) was a remarkable person who achieved great things. His sensitive observations...made history (and) he will always be remembered as the man who revolutionised children's hospitals'. In 1952, Robertson made a film of Laura, a two-year-old girl who had to stay in hospital for eight days for a minor operation and it was this film that influenced Bowlby (and others). During her hospital stay, Laura experienced frequent changes of carer as nurses started and ended their shifts and although Laura saw her mother every day, she was in many respects separated from her primary carer (her mother) throughout her hospital admission.

Laura's reactions to this relatively short separation – she became afraid, upset and withdrawn – were something of a shock to many of Bowlby's contemporaries. Indeed, Bowlby felt that Laura's reactions and the reactions of the many, many other children he observed could not be explained by contemporary theories of child development. For example, some theorists believed that children would form a bond with any adult who met their need for basic essentials such as water, food and physical comfort. Therefore, the attachment relationship a child appeared to form with one or two particular primary carers, such as their mother or father, was considered to be secondary to the mother and father's fulfilment of these basic needs. However, Bowlby realized that if this were true, children such as Laura should not experience such distress when separated from their primary carers, as long as their primary needs continued to be met. However, the 1952 film clearly showed that despite being physically well cared for by her nurses, this in no way ameliorated Laura's suffering at the separation from her mother. Hence, Bowlby began to develop a new theory, drawing from fields such as cognitive psychology, control systems theory, developmental psychology, ethology and evolutionary biology, in order to provide a better explanation for this important aspect of children's behaviour. Bowlby's genius can be seen in his ability to synthesize such a wide range of diverse theoretical concepts and observations and to generate the foundations of a new and coherent theoretical framework.

Interestingly, in addition to drawing on *evolutionary insights* for the development of attachment theory, Bowlby also had a great respect and admiration for Charles Darwin, both as an individual and as a fellow scientist. In his biography of Darwin, Bowlby (1991) writes of Darwin's frequent ill health and explores the idea that these various illnesses were more likely to have been psychological than organic in origin. As the founder of attachment theory, it was perhaps natural that Bowlby would wonder whether these psychological difficulties had their roots in Darwin's childhood, and particularly whether they were related to the death of Darwin's mother when he was eight years old. It is further interesting to compare Bowlby's biographical interest in Charles Darwin with the biographical information we have regarding Bowlby himself. As a child growing up in an upper-middle class English family in the early part of the twentieth century, Bowlby was essentially raised in his early years, not by his mother and father, but by a nanny. When Bowlby was four, his nanny left his family's employ and Bowlby was never to see her again. He later described this separation as 'tragic' and compared it to the loss of his mother. It is of course speculation to wonder whether Bowlby's lifelong interest in the suffering of young children because of separation and loss may have resulted from his own experiences, at least in part.

KEY TEXTS

- Bowlby, J. (1991) *Charles Darwin: A New Life* (New York: W. W. Norton & Company)
- Holmes, J. and Holmes, J. (2014) *John Bowlby and Attachment Theory.* 2nd edn (London: Routledge)
- Van Dijken, S. (1998) *John Bowlby: His Early Life, A Biographical Journey into the Roots of Attachment Theory* (London: Free Association Books)

C

Child Attachment Interview

SEE ALSO Adult Attachment Interview; measures of attachment; research methods in attachment

The Child Attachment Interview (CAI), developed in 2003 by Mary Target, Peter Fonagy and Yael Shmueli-Goetz, is a way of assessing attachment relationships in middle childhood (ages approximately 8–13-years of age). The CAI was developed in response to a perceived 'measurement gap' in the study of attachment relationships for this group of children. The measures that already existed for younger children were either behavioural (as with the *Strange Situation Procedure*) or representational (as with *Story Stem Completion*), in contrast to the *Adult Attachment Interview*, which is a more direct method (in terms of its administration, if not in the analysis and coding). There was and still remains some debate about the age at which it is most helpful to move from representational *measures of attachment* to more direct measures. The CAI, being based on the Adult Attachment Interview, falls squarely into the 'direct measure' category, although it is less complex, comprising 17 questions (as opposed to 20 in the adult interview). Several of the questions are also less complex in terms of their content. For example, in the Adult Attachment Interview, respondents are asked to choose five adjectives or words to describe their childhood relationships whereas in the CAI, the respondent is asked for three adjectives.

The CAI is also conceptually different in one key respect because it seeks to measure and explore the current attachment relationships of the child being interviewed and it does so by asking contemporaneous questions. The Adult Attachment Interview also seeks to measure and explore the adult's current state of mind with regards to attachment but it does so in large part by asking questions about the past and how the adult thinks their past experiences have influenced who they are in the present.

As with the Strange Situation Procedure and the Adult Attachment Interview, the CAI also needs to be completed and analysed by a trained coder in order for a child to be assigned a reliable attachment classification. For the CAI, the classification is based on the Ainsworth–Main attachment patterns of *secure attachment, ambivalent-resistant attachment, avoidant attachment* and *disorganized attachment*. When analysing a CAI, the coder is required to consider nine scales – emotional openness, balance, use of examples, involving anger, idealization, dismissal, conflict resolution, coherence and level of insecurity. The coder assigns the interviewee a score between 1 and 9 for each scale. For example, in regards to emotional openness, a '9' would indicate a very emotionally open child and a '1' would indicate a child who presented no evidence of emotional openness. The coder then uses the scale scores in order to generate an overall attachment classification for the child.

The available evidence suggests that 'The CAI correlates as expected with other attachment measures and...that the CAI is a reliable, valid and promising measure of child-parent attachment in middle childhood' (Shmueli-Goetz *et al.*, 2008, p. 939).

KEY TEXTS

- Allen, J. and Miga, E. (2010) 'Attachment in Adolescence: A Move to the Level of Emotion Regulation', *Journal of Social and Personal Relationships*, 27 (2): pp. 181–190
- Shmueli-Goetz, Y., Target, M., Fonagy, P. and Datta, A. (2008) 'The Child Attachment Interview: A Psychometric Study of Reliability and Discriminant Validity', *Developmental Psychology*, 44 (4): pp. 939–956
- Target, M., Fonagy, P. and Shmueli-Goetz, Y. (2003) 'Attachment Representations in School-Age Children: The Development of the Child Attachment Interview (CAI)', *Journal of Child Psychotherapy*, 29 (2): pp. 171–186

child maltreatment

SEE ALSO **disorganized attachment; neglected children; risk and resilience factors; unresolved loss and trauma**

Most children who are maltreated will develop a form of *insecure attachment*. For some, this could be an organized but insecure pattern, such as *avoidant attachment* or *ambivalent-resistant attachment*. However, a significant number of maltreated children will also display *disorganized attachment* behaviour. Indeed, being maltreated is one of the most common reasons why a child might display disorganized attachment behaviour and maltreated children are more likely to be insecure or to display disorganized attachment behaviour than other 'at risk' children, such as those living in extreme poverty (Cyr *et al.*, 2010). In essence, this is what maltreatment means for many children – being frightened of the person who is meant to love and care for you. As a result, very few maltreated children are able to form a *secure attachment* to the maltreating carer.

As *Bowlby* worked on the development of attachment theory, he was mindful of the fact that maltreatment by an attachment figure would present a unique difficulty for the child and for their attachment systems. Bowlby understood that the attachment system probably evolved in response to the need that human infants have to obtain and maintain proximity with a small number of *adult attachment* figures when they feel distressed or threatened. Unlike many other animals, when they are very young human infants cannot physically follow their carers or protect themselves very easily and they rely on adults for comfort and protection for many, many years of their childhood. This may explain why human infants use *proximity-seeking and safe-haven behaviours*, such as calling out or crying to their attachment figures in order to attract their attention. Thus, the dilemma that parental maltreatment may cause for children is that the attachment figure to whom they would normally approach for comfort and protection is the same person causing them to feel frightened and distressed. Thus, the threat caused by the maltreatment will activate the child's attachment system and cause the child to want to attain proximity with their attachment figure. However, if the attachment figure is the source of the threat, the child's 'fight or flight' behavioural system will also activate with the aim of moving away from the attachment figure or even potentially trying to attack (or control) them before they can cause any (further) harm. When observing children in the Strange Situation Procedure with an abusive attachment figure, this dilemma may be demonstrated in behavioural terms – for example, the child may walk towards the attachment figure in slow motion, they may allow the attachment figure to pick them up but then hit out at them or they may freeze, apparently unable to resolve their twin behavioural goals to move towards and yet simultaneously move away from the attachment figure. Such interactions are indicative of disorganized attachment behaviour although it is important to note that such behaviours are very precisely described and can only be assessed in certain circumstances. Main and Hesse (2000) captured the essence of this dilemma when they described such children as experiencing 'fear without escape (and) fright without solution'. Of course, it is worth noting that children who display disorganized attachment behaviour will also have a secondary (or underlying) classification of avoidant attachment, ambivalent-resistant attachment or even, in a minority of cases, of secure attachment. In other words, disorganized attachment behaviour is not an attachment classification per se but rather a specific behavioural response to a particular frightening or fearful situation and in other situations, the child will tend to organize their attachment behaviour in similar ways to non-maltreated children.

However, child maltreatment is not a simple phenomenon. Most obviously, neglect and abuse are often significantly different and thus the experience of *neglected children* will not necessarily be similar to the experience of abused children. Abuse can be very broadly understood as an adult 'doing something' to the child that causes significant harm. Neglect, on the other hand, can be broadly understood as an adult 'not doing something' that then causes significant harm to the child. In other words, the former is active and the latter is relatively passive (at least in some circumstances). Conceptualized in this way, it is understandable that abuse will usually frighten the child and lead to the display of disorganized attachment behaviour but less clear how neglect would cause the child to feel frightened (depending on why and how the attachment figure was behaving).

Whilst child abuse clearly makes insecure attachment and especially disorganized attachment behaviour more likely, the relationship between different forms of abuse and outcomes for children is very complex. When and for how long the abuse occurs is important, with abuse that takes place over a longer period of time being more likely to lead to persistently negative effects for the child although 'one–off' episodes of abuse can also be very problematic, depending on the nature of the abuse, the identity of the perpetrator and the presence (or absence) of *risk and resilience factors.*

It is also important to bear in mind that whilst physical and sexual abuse may have more 'obvious' and immediate negative effects on children, the experience of neglect and emotional abuse (even in the absence of physical or sexual abuse) is still likely to lead to the child developing an insecure attachment relationship with their primary carers and 'this challenges the assumption that only heinous types of physical abuse or sexual abuse result in negative outcomes for children' (Cyr *et al.*, 2010, p. 143).

KEY TEXTS

- Cicchetti, D. and Carlson, V. (eds) (1989) *Child Maltreatment: Theory and Research on the Causes and Consequences of Child Abuse and Neglect* (Cambridge: Cambridge University Press)
- Cyr, C., Euser, E., Bakermans-Kranenberg, M. and van IJzendoorn, M. (2010) 'Attachment Security and Disorganization in Maltreating and High-Risk Families: A Series of Meta-analyses', *Development and Psychopathology,* 22 (1): pp. 87–108
- Stronach, E., Toth, S., Rogosch, F., Oshri, A., Manly, J. and Cicchetti, D. (2011) 'Child Maltreatment, Attachment Security, and Internal Representations of Mother and Mother–Child Relationships', *Child Maltreatment,* 16 (2): pp. 137–145

criticisms of attachment theory

SEE ALSO **cultural differences; history of attachment theory and research; misuses of attachment theory**

As with any major theory of human development, there are a number of criticisms that have been made of attachment theory. These critical perspectives can be broadly understood as originating from two sources – sociological and particularly feminist criticisms of the underlying principles (and use of) the theory, and criticisms of the empirical basis of the theory.

Some critics of attachment theory argue that it contains an element of 'mother blaming', that it represents a paradigm in which it is the mother's responsibility to ensure the child's optimal development above all else, and that it is the mother who should be held responsible if the child encounters any difficulties. In part, this criticism arises from *Bowlby*'s persistent use of the word 'mother' in his early writings, rather than the more neutral and contemporary terms 'parent', 'primary carer' or 'attachment figure'. There is some validity to this criticism when put in those terms. For example, Bowlby wrote specifically about the effects of 'maternal deprivation' on the child rather than 'paternal deprivation' or any other kind of attachment-related deprivation. In his later writings, Bowlby and others recognized the limitations of this early focus on *mothers* to the exclusion of other potential attachment figures (most obviously *fathers*). In addition, it has become increasingly clear over time that infants can form *multiple attachments* and therefore, the potentially negative effects of loss or separation in relation to one attachment figure may, in some circumstances, be ameliorated by remaining in contact with another. Indeed, having at least one *secure attachment* relationship is one of the clearest protective factors for a child, especially in circumstances where the child's relationship with a second attachment figure is made more difficult, for example, because of the presence of *psychopathology and mental ill health* or *unresolved loss and trauma*.

Another relatively common criticism – in some ways both sociological and empirical – is that attachment theory is deterministic, that it makes the claim that a child's critical early experiences determine their outcomes later in life. It is not clear if attachment theory ever postulated a deterministic model of development but, certainly in contemporary attachment theory, there is no suggestion that the child's early experiences determine later outcomes. Instead, it is more common to refer to 'sensitive periods' of development (rather than critical periods) and as Goldberg has argued:

> One may arrive at many different end points from a given standing point and there are many opportunities to cross from one main limb to another via smaller branches. However, the further out one moves on a particular limb, the less likelihood there is of crossing over to other limbs. (2000, p. 247)

Goldberg's argument is that from any given 'starting point', there are sufficient potential 'end points' so as to render the making of meaningful and accurate individual predictions functionally futile. However, the further one develops along a particular path, the more or less likely different 'end points' become. There is now growing evidence that as the child approaches adolescence, the contribution of *genetic influences* on attachment organization becomes more significant than first thought.

Other criticisms from an empirical perspective include the claim that peer relationships have more influence on adolescents than their relationships with primary carers (Harris, 1999); that various *measures of attachment* are not sufficiently robust; that the infant attachment categories of *avoidant attachment, ambivalent-resistant attachment* and secure attachment are not sufficiently refined; and that attachment categories may not be stable across the lifespan. The common thread of these criticisms is that none of them undermines the basis of attachment theory per se; rather, they offer a critique of certain aspects of it and suggest areas for further research.

KEY TEXTS

• Featherstone, B., White, S. and Morris, K. (2014) *Re-imagining Child Protection: Towards Humane Social Work with Families* (Bristol: The Policy Press), Chapter 4
• Goldberg, S. (2000) *Attachment and Development* (London: Arnold)
• Harris, J. (1999) *The Nurture Assumption* (New York: Touchstone)

Crittenden's Dynamic-Maturational Model

SEE ALSO Bowlby; history of attachment theory and research

Since *Bowlby*'s original work, two alternative models of attachment have developed – the Ainsworth–Main model of ABC-D attachment and Patricia Crittenden's Dynamic-Maturational Model (DMM). Whilst the Ainsworth–Main model has a greater degree of supporting empirical evidence, and hence provides the basis for the majority of attachment research and literature (including this book), nevertheless, the DMM also has an expanding evidence base and is growing in popularity with practitioners.

Whereas the Ainsworth–Main model categorizes infants and children as having either *avoidant attachment* (Type A) relationships, *secure attachment* (Type B) relationships or *ambivalent-resistant attachment* (Type C) relationships, the DMM differs in several ways, notably by including a range of subcategories for Types A, B and C, the omission of *disorganized attachment* (Type D) and the inclusion of two additional Types not found in the Ainsworth–Main model (A/C and AC).

Referring to these various categories as 'Types' stems from early attachment research in which, although it was recognized that infants were exhibiting qualitatively different kinds of attachment behaviour, the nature of the underlying *internal working models* was not yet understood. Hence, early attachment researchers labelled the different kinds of attachment behaviour they saw as A, B and C (and later, D).

However, the key theoretical difference between the two is that the Ainsworth–Main model conceives of safety as being the primary organizing factor for attachment whereas the DMM conceives of danger as the primary organizing factor. Thus, the DMM regards all attachment behaviour as 'organized' in order to maximize the potential for self-protection, including during threatening or anxiety-inducing situations. This difference explains why the DMM does not include the disorganized attachment category because, according to the DMM, all attachment behaviour is adaptive to the environment in which it originated. This is not to say that such behaviour cannot become maladaptive over time as a result of the environment changing but nevertheless, it is a different conception from that of the Ainsworth–Main model.

The DMM also seeks to emphasize the importance of development across the lifespan and to consider how individuals at different stages of maturation are able to protect themselves and, as they grow older, to reproduce and protect any resultant offspring. Thus, patterns of attachment are the organization of mental and behavioural strategies for achieving these (changing) aims. Clearly, as infants develop into children and later into adults, their capacity for increasingly sophisticated mental and behavioural strategies tends to increase although, with regards to *later life attachments*, it may be that they decrease again to a certain extent. Thus, according to the DMM, it follows that the range of available attachment patterns increases over the course of the lifespan, with infants having a more limited number of potential strategies and adults the most. In the full adult DMM model, there are 12 subcategories in total, compared with 7 in the infant version.

Another important concept within the DMM model is the integration (or not) of two different types of information – affect and cognition. Affect refers to feelings or emotions and cognition to mental processes such as learning, language and reasoning. Each of the Types and subcategories within the DMM can be described in terms of the use (and integration) of affective or cognitive information. For example, B3 ('comfortable'), one of the subcategories of Type B (secure attachment), indicates that the individual is able, without distortion, to integrate cognitive and affective information together when making attachment-related decisions (such as 'how should I behave around my carer when I am upset')? On the other hand, A3-4 ('compulsively caregiving/compliant'), one of the subcategories of Type A (avoidant attachment), indicates that the individual tends to rely on 'false positive' affective information. This means they may feign the display of positive emotions as a way of appearing compliant with an attachment figure. As another example, C3-4 ('aggressive/feigned helpless'), one of the subcategories of Type C (ambivalent-resistant attachment), indicates that the individual tends to rely on false cognitive information. This means that they may have distortions within their episodic *memory* of how their attachment figure has responded to displays of attachment behaviour in the past and this distorted information will influence how they behave in the present.

Finally as previously noted, the DMM model contains two Types not represented within the ABC-D model. Type A/C describes individuals who combine two subcategories, one from Type A (avoidant attachment) and one from Type C (ambivalent-resistant attachment). In other words, the A/C Type indicates that the individual combines quite divergent attachment patterns, at times appearing avoidant and at other times ambivalent-resistant. Such individuals will tend to show quite marked shifts in their behaviour as they switch between the two. Type A/C describes individuals who have blended two subcategories, one from Type A and one from Type C, rather than, as with Type A/C, employing them in an alternating manner. Thus, such individuals may show elements of avoidance and ambivalent-resistance at the same time.

In summary, the DMM is a creative and theoretically consistent approach for understanding and interpreting attachment behaviour and patterns across the lifespan. It differs from the arguably more empirically grounded Ainsworth–Main ABC-D model in some significant ways and as such, there is little reason to expect that the models will ever become integrated, as there are simply too many differences between them. Nevertheless, perhaps because of the way the DMM model seems to capture the complexity of close human relationships in a more overt way than the Ainsworth–Main ABC-D model, the DMM has proven to be relatively popular with practitioners (such as clinicians and social workers).

KEY TEXTS

- Crittenden, P. (2006) 'A Dynamic-Maturational Model of Attachment', *Australian and New Zealand Journal of Family Therapy*, 27 (2): pp. 105–115
- Crittenden, P. (2008) *Raising Parents: Attachment Parenting and Child Safety* (London: Routledge)
- Pocock, D. (2010) 'Debating Truth, Error and Distortion in Systemic Psychotherapy. A Contribution from the DMM'. http://www.patcrittenden.com/include/docs/dmm_context_pocock.pdf

cultural differences

SEE ALSO **history of attachment theory and research; measures of attachment**

Many of the early studies of attachment were undertaken using samples of children (and attachment figures) from North American backgrounds and although the pioneering attachment researcher, Mary Ainsworth, ran extensive studies of infants and primary carers in Uganda, nevertheless it is true that the *Strange Situation Procedure* was developed as a measure of infant attachment with middle-class, White populations in the United States of America. This *history of attachment theory and research* raises questions about the general applicability of attachment theory across different cultures and specifically whether *measures of attachment* such as the Strange Situation Procedure or the *Adult Attachment Interview* are valid and reliable when used with children and adults from cultural backgrounds other than middle-class, White and from the USA. For example, in the Strange Situation Procedure, infants experience a number of relatively short separations from their attachment figures followed by episodes of reunion. These separations and reunions are interspersed with separation and reunion episodes with a stranger as well. However, in some cultures, these kinds of separations may be quite typical and therefore less stressful than for infants from middle-class White cultures in the USA. Equally, in cultures where even very brief separations are less typical, infants may find the Strange Situation Procedure to be far more stressful than their day-to-day experiences. If so, such differences may affect how these infants behave during the Strange Situation Procedure and in turn their attachment classifications (although if true this would be a problem with the Strange Situation Procedure rather than of attachment theory per se).

With regards the history of attachment theory and research, as *Bowlby* formulated the theory of attachment, he drew on a number of *evolutionary insights* and argued persuasively that infants have a universal need to attach to a small number of adults (usually primary carers) and as such attachment theory would be applicable across all cultures. However, this is not the same as saying that infants (and older children and adults) will express or experience their attachment relationships in the same way, regardless of culture.

van IJzendoorn and Sagi (1999) debated the cultural context of attachment and identified four key questions:

1. Do infants in all cultures become attached to one or more primary carers (except in situations of extreme developmental *disability*)?
2. Is *secure attachment* the most common category of attachment in all cultures or only in some?
3. Do the same caregiver characteristics (such as *attunement and sensitivity*) affect the quality of infant attachment relationships in all cultures?
4. In relation to infants from the same culture, do those with early secure attachment relationships consistently demonstrate more positive outcomes than those with early *insecure attachment* relationships?

All four of these questions have been answered in the affirmative in relation to most Western cultures where, based on the available evidence, it is possible to conclude with some confidence that (almost) all infants will form attachments to a small number of attachment figures, that the most common category of attachment relationship for children and adults is secure (or secure-autonomous), that certain characteristics (such as attunement and sensitivity) do reliably influence the formation and development of attachment relationships and that children with early secure attachment relationships tend to have consistently more positive outcomes in later life when compared to infants with early insecure attachment relationships. In relation to non-Western cultures, there is much less data available but crucially, none of the available data significantly contradicts these conclusions and much of it is arguably supportive of them.

For example, studies of children raised in communal caregiving arrangements, such as in an Israeli kibbutz or in Efe culture, still form attachment relationships with a small number of adult (or adolescent) carers. This is not to suggest that the development and nature of attachment relationships is unaffected by such communal care environments. Weiss and Shilkret (2010) found that children from Israeli kibbutzim are more likely to develop *ambivalent-resistant attachment* relationships than many other groups of children. Nevertheless, the picture that emerges from the body of cross-cultural attachment research – undertaken in places as diverse as China, Israel, Japan, Kenya, Mexico, Nigeria, Russia, South Korea and Uganda – is that differences between countries (in terms of the distribution of infant attachment patterns) are less significant than the differences found within countries.

In relation to van IJzendoorn and Sagi's second question, there are few studies that have found anything other than that the majority of infants, children and adults have secure attachment relationships or secure states of mind with regards to attachment, despite many of these studies having been undertaken with people living in extremely adverse conditions. Rates of insecure attachment are generally higher in situations of extreme poverty, famine and war (as you might expect) but even in these environments, secure attachments are still usually more common.

In relation to van IJzendoorn and Sagi's third and fourth questions, there is simply less data available. However, the evidence we do have again suggests that caregiver characteristics such as attunement and sensitivity reliably increase the likelihood of a secure attachment relationship developing and that secure attachment relationships in childhood are generally more likely to associate with positive outcomes in later life than insecure attachment relationships.

Overall, there is robust evidence in support of the hypothesis that attachment is a universal human phenomenon and that certain core elements of attachment theory remain consistent across different cultures (such as the prevalence of the secure attachment category). The existence of differences in the distribution of attachment patterns across different cultures should not come as a surprise, given the variety of ways in which people may organize the raising of children. What may be more is surprising is the degree of similarity found between different cultures in terms of the distribution of attachment patterns, given the variety and diversity of human cultural practices.

KEY TEXTS

- Keller, H. (2013) 'Attachment and Culture', *Journal of Cross-Cultural Psychology*, 44: pp. 175–194
- Sroufe, L. A. (2005) Attachment and Development: A Prospective, Longitudinal Study from Birth to Adulthood', *Attachment and Human Development*, 7 (4): pp. 349–367
- van IJzendoorn, M. and Sagi, A. (1999) Cross-cultural Patterns of Attachment: Universal and Contextual Dimensions' in J. Cassidy and P. Shaver (eds), *Handbook of Attachment* (New York: Guilford)

d

disability

SEE ALSO child maltreatment; loss and bereavement; measures of attachment

When considering the attachment relationships of disabled children, one must be careful about attributing any apparent differences (between the attachment relationships and experiences of disabled children and those of non-disabled children) to any individual impairment without first considering whether and how any such differences might be related to broader caregiving and social systems.

Thus, when we consider the research which has found disabled children are more likely to have *insecure attachments* to their attachment figures than non-disabled children, it is right to ask why this might be the case. According to Howe (2006), it is not the impairment of the child that is associated with higher rates of insecurity but rather the interaction between the child and the carer's state of mind with regards to attachment. We would then need to consider why states of mind with regards to attachment might differ between the carers of disabled children and non-disabled children or indeed what might be happening for attachment figures who care for both disabled and non-disabled children. To some degree, any differences must surely relate to social factors rather than individual factors, given that *disability* occurs widely and relatively frequently across and within all social groups. In other words, the attachment figure's state of mind will be influenced not only the different challenges involved in caring for some disabled children but having to do so within a social context of widespread discrimination against and a lack of support for disabled people.

Another issue to consider is the greater likelihood that disabled children will experience *child maltreatment*. We know that child maltreatment is one of the more common reasons why children develop more extreme forms of insecure attachment relationships and we also know that disabled children are more likely to experience abuse and neglect, relatively speaking, than non-disabled children. Stern *et al.* (2000) completed some helpful research in this area that illustrates how some of these social complexities may operate in practice. The authors asked several groups of adults to play with an unfamiliar infant and found that, if they informed the adults that the infant had been born prematurely, they tended to touch the infant less frequently and to demonstrate less enjoyment at interacting with them compared to when they were not given this information. As the child was obviously no different regardless of the information given to the adults, it is possible that the changes in the adults' behaviour related to their pre-existing social constructions of prematurity (and disability), rather than to the child's supposed disability (or not). If true and if representative of actual adult–child dyads, this could help explain the greater likelihood of a child with a disability developing an insecure attachment relationship.

Another perspective that may be applied to attachment and disability is that of *loss and bereavement*. Bowlby (1980) wrote extensively about the grieving process that usually follows the loss of a loved one and about the relationship between grief and attachment. In particular, he observed that when a child's attachment figure dies, the child may react in any or all of the following ways – they may search for their attachment figure, express disbelief that they are really gone, worry that they somehow caused the loss, and experience disorientation in situations where the absent attachment figure was previously present. *Bowlby* argued that this sense of loss would be 'resolved' once the child came to accept it as permanent (contrasting this with *unresolved loss and trauma*). Some researchers have sought to apply this model to the attachment figures of disabled children, arguing that they might feel a sense of loss regarding the 'healthy child' they likely hoped they would have. They also identified similarities between the grieving reactions of some children to the loss of an attachment figure and the reactions of some carers to the birth or diagnosis of a disabled child. For example, Marvin and Pianta (1996) found that carers who were 'resolved' to their child's disability, those who accepted that the child's condition was permanent, were more likely to focus on the child's abilities (rather than impairments) and more likely to develop a *secure attachment* relationship with them. This finding may be said to be similar to the final stage of Bowlby's model of grief, in which the child, by accepting the finality of their loss, achieves resolution. However, the problem with this approach is twofold – firstly, for almost all prospective parents, there will be an 'imagined child' and a real child and there will always be some difference between the two. In other words, the 'gap' between what any parent may hope for and expect before having a child (whether biological or adoptive) may differ from the reality. Thus it is not clear why, for children with a disability, the experience would best be described as a form of 'loss'. Secondly, it is in our view unhelpful to compare the loss (i.e. the death) of an attachment figure with the experience of *parenting* a child with a disability – clearly, in the latter case, there is a living child, growing in a complex way, and although the experience of not reaching (or a delay in reaching) 'normal' developmental milestones may be significant for some – and may involve a degree of sadness and grief – it is an ongoing process and therefore quite different from, and unrelated to, the experience of the permanent loss of an attachment figure.

KEY TEXTS
- Bowlby, J. (1980) *Attachment and Loss, Volume 3: Loss, Sadness and Depression* (New York: Basic Books)
- Howe, D. (2006) 'Disabled Children, Parent–Child Interaction and Attachment', *Child and Family Social Work*, 11 (2): pp. 95–106
- Marvin, R. and Pianta, R. (1996) 'Mother's Reactions to their Child's Diagnosis: Relations with Security of Attachment', *Journal of Clinical Child Psychology*, 25 (4): pp. 436–445

disorganized attachment

SEE ALSO **(reactive) attachment disorder; child maltreatment; neglected children**

In early experiments regarding the attachment relationships of young children, Mary Ainsworth and others encountered a number of children whose behaviour could not be easily classified via the *Strange Situation Procedure.* For the majority of children, Ainsworth found their behaviour could be categorized as representing *secure attachment, ambivalent-resistant attachment* or *avoidant attachment*. However, for a minority of children, although they tended to behave like other children when the attachment figure left the room and in the presence of a stranger, they seemed to behave oddly when their attachment figure returned. Ainsworth (and others) saw children who, on reunion with their attachment figure, would begin to approach them but then stop suddenly in their tracks and stay still for 15–20 seconds; or they would approach the attachment figure whilst holding up their hands in front of their face. One child was observed to walk towards the attachment figure whilst turning their head the other way and quite a few sank to the floor and remained still for some time, motionless and apparently 'frozen'. Lyons-Ruth and Jacobvitz describe more recent examples:

> One unclassifiable infant, for example, cried loudly while attempting to gain her mother's lap, then suddenly fell silent and stopped moving for several seconds. Others were observed: rocking on hands and knees following an abortive approach; moving away from the parent to the wall when apparently frightened by the stranger; screaming by the door upon separation from the parent and then moving silently away upon reunion; raising hand to mouth in an apprehensive gesture immediately upon seeing the parent; and, while in an apparently good mood, swiping at the parent's face with a trancelike expression. (2008, p. 676)

Ainsworth, as a meticulous researcher, recorded the behaviour of these children as 'unclassified' and began to enquire into their early histories. Over time, it became apparent that many of these children had been abused or neglected or there were suggestions or unsubstantiated concerns about *child maltreatment*. However, it was not until the early 1990s that Mary Main and Judith Solomon began to analyse the behaviour of these children more systematically. Main and Solomon studied 200 tapes of children displaying this kind of behaviour in the Strange Situation Procedure and developed the idea of a fourth primary type of attachment behaviour, which came to be known as disorganized attachment behaviour. Again, Lyons-Ruth and Jacobvitz (2008) describe some examples:

> unclassified infants were observed approaching the parent with head averted; rocking on hands and knees following an abortive

approach; or screaming by the door for the parent, then moving away on reunion. What unclassified infants appeared to have in common were contradictory intentions (approaching a parent with head averted), or behaviours that involved apprehension, either directly (fearful facial expressions, oblique approaches), or indirectly (e.g. disoriented behaviours, including dazed or trance-like expressions; or freezing of all movement at the parent's entrance). (2008, p. 676)

Note the 'shutting down' quality of these behaviours, denoting 'fear without solution'. Such behaviour was identified in about 10–15 per cent of the children studied (see Out, Bakermans-Kranenburg and van IJzendoorn, 2009); but this figure rises to between 50 and 80 per cent of children who have been maltreated.

The phrase 'fear without solution' captures the central paradox of disorganized attachment behaviour, the child's overwhelming sense of fear caused by an attachment figure at times when they 'should' be providing the child with comfort and protection. It may also be the case that the child arouses the attachment figure's own 'fear system', possibly by triggering painful *memory*, especially of *unresolved loss and trauma*, which are then projected onto the child – in either case, the impact on the child is that the attachment figure is not a source of comfort for them and hence the child's *proximity-seeking and safe-haven behaviours* becomes disrupted by a concurrent need to protect themselves from the threat posed by the attachment figure.

Understanding this experience of fear is important in understanding the experience of children who display disorganized attachment behaviour and it is somewhat different from more familiar experiences of fear. Consider, for example, how you might feel if you found yourself in a maze and gradually realized that you have no way out. Imagine your growing sense of panic as it becomes more and more obvious that you are trapped. Alternatively, imagine entering a supposedly haunted room and accepting a bet to stay the whole night. Even the toughest and most hardened rationalist is likely to become troubled by fearful thoughts and to find his or her imagination 'running away' in response to noises in the dark. But this is not like the kind of fear experienced by the very young child presenting with disorganized attachment behaviour. His or her fear is characterized by a lack of preparedness, even an absence of fore-boding. This child is stuck, knowing they can neither (effectively) flee from the attachment figure, nor can they rely on the attachment figure to help them manage the fear through the provision of comfort and protection.

It is also important to note that disorganized attachment behaviour is only observed in infants and toddlers for a short time, during situations in which they are feeling frightened of their attachment figure and in which they would otherwise seek comfort from them. In most other situations, the child's behaviour may appear quite similar to that of any other child. In older children, aged four or five and older, the child may display other kinds of behaviour towards an attachment figure who frightens them. For example, they may act 'punitively' towards them, by showing hostile or directive behaviour, typically through the use of harsh commands, verbal threats or physical aggression. Alternatively, they may display overtly 'caring' behaviour, perhaps appearing excessively cheery, polite or helpful. These kinds of behavioural strategies are typically developed as a way of maintaining some kind of (non-frightening) engagement with the attachment figure and do not indicate that the child is no longer afraid.

A very large number of studies on the developmental origins of disorganized attachment behaviour followed swiftly from the research of Mary Main and her associates (Main and Weston, 1981), as well as a number of systematic reviews by Marinus van IJzendoorn and his colleagues at the University of Leiden in the Netherlands. These studies include a growing and reliable index of key correlates and consequences of disorganized attachment, including whether there might be some *genetic influences*. The longer-term consequences of prolonged experiences of disorganized attachment behaviour in childhood are usually negative and may include problems such as an increased risk of physical ill health (because of the effects of prolonged and heightened stress on the body), *dissociation* and dissociative behaviour, controlling, external-izing or aggressive behaviour, conduct and attention disorders and difficulties related to *psychopathology and mental ill health*, such as Borderline Personality Disorder (BPD). Children who present with disorganized attachment behaviour are also more likely to develop symptoms of depression to a clinically relevant degree in later life, to exhibit hostile behaviour towards their peers and to present with social and school phobias.

The experience of fear without solution may also be present for children who are frightened 'for' their parent (as distinct from being frightened of their parent). This scenario is very different from child abuse as perhaps typically conceptualised (e.g. physical or sexual abuse) and will include experiences such as witnessing or hearing domestic abuse (a situation that is increasingly recognised – rightly in our opinion – as distinctively emotionally abusive for a child). In such cases, whilst the child's parents may not behave in a directly abusive way towards the child (e.g. the child may suffer no direct physical or sexual abuse), the child will nevertheless often become fearful 'for' the victim/survivor (usually the mother) and especially in the presence of the perpetrator.

Finally, more recent research suggests there may exist qualitatively different types of disorganized attachment behaviour (see Padrón, Carlson and Sroufe, 2014). For example, there seems to be a marked difference between 'stilling and freezing' behaviours compared to 'simultaneously approaching and avoiding' the caregiver.

KEY TEXTS
- Padrón, E., Carlson, E. A. and Sroufe, L. A. (2014) 'Frightened Versus Not Frightened Disorganized Infant Attachment: Newborn Characteristics and Maternal Caregiving', *American Journal of Orthopsychiatry*, 84 (2): pp. 201–208
- Shemmings, D. and Shemmings, Y. (2011) *Understanding Disorganized Attachment: Theory and Practice for Working with Children and Adults* (London: Jessica Kingsley Publishers)
- Shemmings, D. and Shemmings, Y. (eds) (2014) *Assessing Disorganized Attachment Behaviour in Children: An Evidence-based Model for Understanding and Supporting Families* (London: Jessica Kingsley Publishers)

dissociation

SEE ALSO **disorganized attachment; memory; unresolved loss and trauma**

Dissociation is similar in some ways to the experience of being unable to register your conscious mind, becoming disconnected from your own sensory perceptions, from your working *memory*, and from your own thoughts and feelings. However, dissociation refers to more severe detachments from physical and emotional experiences, and may occur in response to traumatic events or memories of *unresolved loss and trauma*. In severe cases, repeated dissociations may result in a diagnosis of Dissociative Identity Disorder (DID). Although rates of diagnosis for dissociative disorders are relatively low, this may reflect under-diagnosis rather than low prevalence. The causes of dissociative disorders are not well understood but one of the most common presumed antecedents is childhood trauma, such as *child maltreatment*, especially when the trauma is unresolved. However, non-traumatized individuals can experience unbidden dissociation as well and not all traumatized individuals experience dissociation. This suggests there are other antecedents or mediating factors in addition to or as an alternative to childhood trauma.

One possible factor is the nature of the child's early caregiving environment. Inconsistent caregiving, high levels of harsh discipline, increased exposure to risk and dissociation in childhood attachment figures have all been linked with higher levels of dissociation in adulthood. These findings suggest a potential link between dissociation and attachment and indeed it has been suggested that DID might be better conceptualized as an example of an *attachment disorder* because of the similarity between the behaviour of children who experience the sudden loss of an attachment figure and the extreme detachment and emotional unresponsiveness of adults with DID. There are also similarities between the behaviour of children demonstrating *disorganized attachment* behaviour and dissociative behaviour in later life and it is well established that child maltreatment is one of the most common causal reasons for disorganized attachment. Children who present with disorganized attachment behaviour are thought to experience a 'breakdown' of their typical attachment behaviour, underpinned by an inability – at a particular moment in time – to integrate two systems of behaviour, attachment (with the aim of increasing proximity with an attachment figure) and 'fight-or-flight' (with the aim of attacking or moving away from the attachment figure). Children who experience this kind of dilemma may end up lacking a coherent sense of self as a result of their inability to integrate these two very different perceptions of the same attachment figure and this again suggests a link with the dissociative experience of being unaware of one's own perceptions, memories, thoughts and feelings. Although disorganized attachment behaviour in childhood may not cause dissociation in adulthood, there is some evidence to suggest that it is a precursor of it.

In addition to this link between disorganized attachment in childhood and dissociation in later life, when the attachment figures of children who present with disorganized attachment take part in an *Adult Attachment Interview*, they tend to be far less coherent in their answers and are far more likely to be categorized as 'unresolved' with regards to trauma or loss than most other adults and there are notable similarities between the ways in which unresolved loss and trauma are identified or evidenced via the Adult Attachment Interview and clinical signs of dissociation. Indeed, so related are the three concepts of trauma, dissociation and disorganized attachment that they have been described as 'three strands of a single braid' (Liotti, 2004). Other studies have considered what might link the unresolved status of adults (as coded using the Adult Attachment Interview) and disorganized attachment behaviour in children and this has given rise to the hypothesis that when an adult experiences unresolved loss and trauma, this may lead to the display of frightened or frightening (FR) behaviour towards the child. Further studies have refined our understanding of the ways in which FR behaviour can be exhibited – as frightened behaviour, threatening behaviour or dissociative behaviour.

The kinds of dissociative behaviour that might result in a child feeling 'frightened of' or 'frightened for' their attachment figure includes trance-like states and altered or anomalous facial and vocal expressions. From a young child's perspective, an attachment figure who at times of heightened stress, at the precise time when the child's attachment system is activated, begins to act in dissociative ways, becoming at the very least unavailable for the child if not actively frightening, is likely to be experienced by the child as highly anxiety-provoking. As this occurs at a time when the child is already anxious, this can lead to a situation in which the child's attachment system is frequently activated but only rarely or inconsistently responded to. In theoretical terms, one would expect this to lead to the development of an *insecure attachment* and in more extreme situations, to disorganized attachment behaviour and indeed, this is what many studies have found. Thus, dissociation has a potentially powerful role in the *trans-generational transmission* of attachment and especially for more insecure and disorganized forms of attachment behaviour.

KEY TEXTS

- Bremner, J. and Marmar, C. (eds) (1998) *Trauma, Memory and Dissociation* (Washington, DC: American Psychiatric Press)
- Liotti, G. (2004) 'Trauma, Dissociation, and Disorganization: Three Strands of a Single Braid', *Psychotherapy: Theory, Research, Practice, Training,* 41 (4): pp. 472–486
- Rassin, E. and van Rootselaar, A. (2006) 'From Dissociation to Trauma? Individual Differences in Dissociation as Predictor of "Trauma" Perception', *Journal of Behavior Therapy and Experimental Psychiatry,* 37 (2): pp. 127–139

e

'earned' (or 'acquired') security

SEE ALSO **Adult Attachment Interview; internal working models; secure attachment**

Whether or not attachment patterns are continuous and stable over time remains an important question for attachment researchers. Although attachment security (or insecurity) is conceptualized as being a quality of particular attachment relationships, rather than as an individual trait or aspect of *temperament*, nevertheless attachment theory predicts an individual's attachment pattern will stay fairly consistent over time (assuming a consistent caregiving environment). This is not to say, for example, that a child will always exhibit the same attachment behaviour but it does suggest that the underlying approach or strategy for dealing with attachment-related anxiety and stress will tend to remain the same and there is some evidence to support this view. For example, Fraley *et al.* (2011) measured attachment representations over a 30-day time period with one group of adults and over a year with another group. They found that despite temporary variations in attachment, there were stable, underpinning factors for both groups. Other studies have looked at the continuity and stability of attachment patterns between childhood and adolescence and found that infant attachment classification is a significant predictor of adolescent attachment classification in the majority of cases. *Bowlby* alluded to this stability when he discussed his idea of *internal working models* of attachment but he also envisaged that any changes in these internal working models would relate to the presence and timing of positive and negative (attachment-related) life events. So although early childhood experiences of attachment are important for the formation of internal working models and many individuals' attachment patterns remain stable over time, it would be incorrect to suppose that childhood attachment and *adult attachment* are always continuous or that the nature and quality of a person's attachment relationships are ever fixed. Whilst stability and continuity may be the norm for many, there is an important concept within attachment theory known as 'lawful discontinuity'. Discontinuity refers simply to any situation in which a person's attachment pattern changes significantly over time. 'Lawful' refers to the idea that the reasons for the discontinuity – the significant change in the attachment pattern – are consistent with the wider body of attachment theory. In other words, if a child's attachment pattern was found to have changed significantly over time despite no significant changes in their caregiving environment or attachment relationships, this would be an unexpected ('unlawful') change from the perspective of attachment theory – why should a child significantly alter the ways in which they respond to attachment-related situations of anxiety if their attachment figures are essentially behaving in the same ways as before? Lawful discontinuity, on the other hand, refers to situations in which a person changes their attachment patterns, but only when these changes are preceded by significant changes in their caregiving environment or attachment relationships (although more recent research regarding adolescent attachment challenges some of these assumptions, suggesting that *genetic influences* become more important in the teenage years).

One of the more common situations of lawful discontinuity is when, as a child, a person has an *insecure attachment* relationship with one or more attachment figures, but as an adult the same person is categorized with a secure 'frame of mind'. This example of lawful discontinuity is known as 'earned' or 'acquired' security. One of the potential difficulties with this is that the Adult Attachment Interview is not designed to explore what actually happened in a person's childhood but to understand their perceptions of what happened, a quite different thing. Whether adults categorized as earned secure actually have had more difficult childhoods is not easy to discern but even so, learning more about the process of earned security is clearly very valuable, not only in terms of extending our understanding of attachment but also in understanding how maltreated or *neglected children* might be able to develop security in their attachment relationships later in life. Nevertheless, as alluded to above, actually studying adults categorized as earned secure is very challenging – identifying earned security via the Adult Attachment Interview may be relatively simple (for suitably trained coders) but to study retrospectively what led to this change in attachment organization is more difficult. Equally, identifying infants with insecure attachments via the *Strange Situation Procedure* is relatively simple (for suitably trained coders) but only a minority of them will present with earned security in later life.

Roisman *et al.* (2002) have undertaken research in this challenging area and did so by using data from a longitudinal study conducted over 23 years. They found that adults categorized as earned secure reported slightly more distressing childhood experiences than those categorized as (continuous) 'secure' (i.e. adults who were rated as secure in the present and as having had *secure attachments* in childhood), but they queried whether these adults had actually encountered more distressing childhood experiences or whether they simply recalled them as having been more distressing. In other words, although many of the adults categorized as earned secure believed they had had more distressing childhoods than (continuous) 'secure' adults, Roisman *et al.* queried whether this was necessarily the case. Indeed, they found that earned secure adults described some of the most supportive maternal care found within the study, although they themselves did not perceive it as such. These findings serve to underline the point that the Adult Attachment Interview is an instrument for examining an adult's perception of early childhood and not necessarily the reality of it.

KEY TEXTS

- Fraley, R. C., Vicary, A., Brumbaugh, C. and Roisman, G. (2011) 'Patterns of Stability in Adult Attachment: An Empirical Test of Two Models of Continuity and Change', *Journal of Personality and Social Psychology*, 101 (5): pp. 974–992

- Pearson, J. (1994) 'Earned- and Continuous-Security in Adult Attachment: Relation to Depressive Symptomatology and Parenting Style', *Development and Psychopathology*, 6 (2): pp. 359–373

- Roisman, G. *et al.* (2002) 'Earned-Secure Attachment Status in Retrospect and Prospect', *Child Development*, 73 (4): pp. 1204–1219

emotion (or 'affect') regulation

SEE ALSO **attunement and sensitivity; mentalization and reflective function**

The phrase 'affect regulation' is used in a variety of different ways and as such lacks a consistent meaning. Gross (1999, p. 275) provides one possible definition, namely that affect regulation is the process 'by which individuals influence which emotions they have, when they have them, and how they experience and express these emotions'. This definition, whilst relatively clear, overlooks the role of close relationships, especially attachment relationships, in the development of affect regulation. Thompson (1994, pp. 27–28) gives a more expansive definition, arguing that affect regulation 'consists of the extrinsic and intrinsic processes responsible for monitoring, evaluating and modifying emotional reactions, especially their intensive and temporal features, to accomplish one's goals'. Fonagy *et al.* (2004), in their discussion of *mentalization and reflective function*, argue that affect regulation operates on many levels, including neuro-chemically, operating like other homeostatic functions in seeking to maintain (emotional) equilibrium. In some cases, such neurobiological affect regulation is amenable to a 'willed choice', such as when a nervous actor prior to an opening night performance 'forces' herself to feel calm by consciously breathing more slowly. This ability to consciously regulate one's own affect brings us into the realm of 'mentalized affectivity', that is, the ability to be conscious of an affective state whilst still experiencing it.

Affect regulation is a central component of contemporary attachment theory, with Shore and Shore (2008, p. 9) arguing that 'attachment theory (is) a regulation theory'. By this they mean that recent neurobiological insights have enabled attachment researchers to understand how early relationships between an infant and an attachment figure may significantly impact on the development of the infant's capacity for self-regulation in later life. This process appears to happen via the *attunement and sensitivity* of the infant's attachment figure. For example, many attachment figures will help the infant to regulate his or her emotions by demonstrating an understanding not only of what the infant is feeling but by making reasonable assumptions as to the cause. This can include mirroring and amplifying the infant's positive affect, such as joy, happiness or pleasant surprise, as well as helping to manage more negative affect, such as sadness, upset or anger. Shore and Shore have also argued that just as attunement is important, so is the 'recovery' from moments of misattunement. In other words, it is unrealistic to expect that the child's attachment figure will be attuned all of the time and indeed, even the most sensitive attachment figures seem to 'get it wrong' about half the time. Thus, recognizing misattunement with the child is arguably as important for the development of affect regulation as moments of attunement, in part because such misattunements offer the child an opportunity to learn about interactive repair.

KEY TEXTS

- Fonagy, P., Gergely, G., Jurist, E. and Target, M. (2004) *Affect Regulation, Mentalization, and the Development of the Self* (London: Karnac Books)
- Gross, J. (1999) 'Emotion Regulation: Past, Present and Future', *Cognition and Emotion*, 13 (5): pp. 551–573
- Thompson, R. (1994) 'Emotion Regulation: A Theme in Search of a Definition' in N. Fox (ed.), 'The Development of Emotion Regulation: Biological and Behavioural Considerations', *Monographs of the Society for Research in Child Development*, 59 (2–3): pp. 225–252

evolutionary insights

SEE ALSO **genetic influences; Harlow's monkey experiments; history of attachment theory and research**

When *Bowlby* first developed attachment theory, he was inspired by evidence and ideas from a range of disciplines including psychology and psychotherapy but also from fields such as ethology and evolutionary biology. Indeed, it is possible to conceptualize attachment theory as being a subset of evolutionary biology rather than as a psychological theory per se (see Bell, 2012). Bowlby and other researchers noted that within the animal kingdom as a whole, humans (and a number of other primates and animals, such as those included in *Harlow's monkey experiments*) are born seemingly 'before they are ready'. For example, human infants cannot walk for many months after they are born and many will not learn to walk with any degree of stability until they are at least one year of age. Human infants cannot physically seek out sources of nourishment for themselves and without the care and protection of an older human (usually their mother and/or father but potentially any adult with an interest in caring for them) they have almost no hope of survival.

Given the vulnerability of newborn babies, one would expect that the process of evolution by natural selection would very quickly ensure the rapid spread of any genetic mutations that increased the likelihood of adults providing care and protection to infants and young children during the most vulnerable periods of their life.[1] This may explain why babies have certain physical features such as large eyes, small noses and small mouths, features that are almost universally seen as 'cute' (indeed, babies' eyes are so large that they usually reach their full adult size by three months of age, whilst the rest of the baby's facial features take much longer to 'catch up'). However, in addition to their physical features, Bowlby theorized that the formation of attachment bonds between the more vulnerable infant and the stronger, more capable adult was another method by which natural selection 'worked' in order to increase the infant's chances of survival.

What we find with human infants is that despite their significant vulnerability postpartum (when compared with most other mammals), they are born with the crucial and innate ability to relate to adults from birth. However, attachment is not the same as imprinting, a process that some animals go through, in which a baby animal will bond with (imprint upon) the first adult of the same species (or sometimes even of another species) they see. Instead, human infants have the capacity to form an attachment relationship with any adult from whom they receive consistent care and attention over time and, rather than going through a critical period of development, human infants experience sensitive periods in which they are 'primed' to form attachment relationships but after which the capacity to form attachments still remains, even across the lifespan.

Finally, taking an evolutionary perspective on attachment leads to the (rather speculative but intriguing) possibility that although in all populations studied to date, the majority of people can be categorized into the three organized categories of *secure attachment*, *avoidant attachment* and *ambivalent-resistant attachment*, there may have been periods of time in the past when other categories or attachment patterns may have emerged and disappeared again, depending on the contextual environmental conditions. And, thus, there could be others that may develop in future (albeit over evolutionary time frames rather than human ones).

KEY TEXTS

- Bell, D. (2012) *The Dynamics of Connection: How Evolution and Biology Create Caregiving and Attachment* (Plymouth, England: Lexington Books)
- Music, G. (2010) *Nurturing Natures: Attachment and Childhood Emotion* (Abingdon: Psychology Press)
- Simpson, J. and Belsky, J. (2006) 'Attachment Theory within a Modern Evolutionary Framework' in J. Cassidy and P. Shaver (eds), *Handbook of Attachment: Theory, Research and Clinical Implications.* 2nd edn (London: Guilford Press): pp. 131–157

NOTE

1. Discussing evolutionary theory in terms of 'purpose' can be very misleading – of course, evolution by natural selection is not a teleological process and as such, has no purpose, design or goals. However, as an analogy, it can be useful (if only for the sake of brevity) to talk about evolution by natural selection 'as if' it were working purposefully. Furthermore, it is of course unlikely that attachment and caregiving behaviours evolved after the speciation of humans from the wider ape family – rather, these behaviours were presumably inherited from our common ancestor with other primates who also demonstrate similar behaviour.

exploration and security

SEE ALSO **insecure attachment; proximity-seeking and safe-haven behaviours; secure attachment**

There are two fundamental components to any attachment relationship. If we use, as an example, the relationship between an infant and their attachment figure, these two fundamental components are, firstly, the infant's use of the attachment figure as a safe haven, someone to whom they can direct *proximity-seeking and safe-haven behaviours* during situations of increased anxiety; and secondly, the infant's use of the attachment figure as a *secure base* from which to explore. Although here we have used the example of a child–adult dyad, these components also apply to *adult attachment* relationships, including *romantic attachments.*

When observing infants in the *Strange Situation Procedure*, it is possible to see how infants behave differently towards their attachment figures upon or during episodes of reunion and it is typically their behaviour at times of reunion that leads to their overall categorization as either having *secure attachment* or *insecure attachment* relationships. However, in addition to these differences, it is also possible to observe other differences in the ways in which infants in the Strange Situation Procedure will explore, how they play with the toys and interact with the stranger when their attachment figure is present. Children with secure attachment relationships will tend to explore with more freedom and independence than children with insecure attachment relationships, especially following the first episode of separation, after which these children will tend to inhibit their exploration to a greater degree than children with secure attachment relationships. This framework of greater security enabling greater independent exploration and engagement can also be applied to adults. Romano, Fitzpatrick and Janzen (2008) investigated the security of the relationship between 59 adults and their counsellors, seeking to find whether adults who rated themselves as more secure (based on *self-report measures of attachment*) would also feel more able to engage in 'in-session' explorations with the counsellor. In this sense, exploration was taken to mean exploring therapeutic issues with the counsellor rather than the kind of exploratory play seen in the Strange Situation Procedure with infants. Nevertheless, what Romano and colleagues found seems to support the idea that the concept of the secure base does have some relevance for adult-to-adult counselling relationships, particularly because they found a positive correlation between the adult's self-reported experience of attachment security with the counsellor and the level of depth they felt able to achieve in the sessions.

Interestingly, the relationship between felt security and a greater ability to explore might also have some resonance in the field of religious faith as well. Using a method known as the 'Attachment to God Inventory' (similar in nature to the Experiences in Close Relationships Scale, and one of a group of self-report measures of attachment), Beck (2006) found that individuals of the Christian faith who feel that God provides them with something akin to a secure base appear more able to engage in theological explorations and are more tolerant of individuals with a different form of Christian faith (e.g. Catholic rather than Protestant) than those who reported less security in their relationship with God. Taken together, these and other findings suggest there might be something fundamental about the relationship between exploration and security across a range of different relational circumstances.

From the perspective of an infant with an insecure attachment relationship in the Strange Situation Procedure, especially after they have experienced the first episode of separation, they face something of a dilemma (a resolvable dilemma, but a dilemma, nonetheless). The infant is now aware that their attachment figure is prepared to leave them alone (either with or without the stranger) and this causes them to feel anxious, triggering their attachment system. A child with an *avoidant attachment* relationship with the attachment figure has learned they need to 'downplay' their anxiety in order to increase the likelihood the attachment figure will stay with them (or at least not reject them). For these infants, they tend to find it difficult to return to exploratory behaviour because they are more concerned to monitor the attachment figure for any signs that they might leave again. Therefore, whilst they may appear superficially to return to playful activity, it is actually their attachment system that remains active rather than their exploratory system of behaviour. For an infant with an *ambivalent-resistant attachment* relationship to the attachment figure, it is perhaps more obvious that they have not re-activated their exploratory behaviour because, after a period of separation, they will tend to 'overdo' their anxiety even if the attachment figure does offer some comfort. The behaviour of infants from both of these groups indicates that the attachment figure has not been able to soothe the infant nor to reassure them they will not leave them feeling anxious again in the near future. This is in contrast to infants with secure attachment relationships to their attachment figure, who tend to return to playing with the toys relatively quickly without any of the wary watchfulness of infants with insecure attachment relationships. These infants are demonstrating they have confidence in the ability of the attachment figure to soothe them (again) should they become anxious a second or third time, and it is this confidence in the availability and ability of the attachment figure to help that allows for a greater degree of independent exploration.

KEY TEXTS

- Bowlby, J. (2005) *A Secure Base* (London: Routledge Classics)
- Holmes, J. (2001) *The Search for the Secure Base: Attachment Theory and Psychotherapy* (New York: Routledge)
- Romano, V., Fitzpatrick, M. and Janzen, J. (2008) 'The Secure-base Hypothesis: Global Attachment, Attachment to Counsellor and Session Exploration in Psychotherapy', *Journal of Counselling and Psychology*, 55 (4): pp. 495–504

f

fathers

SEE ALSO **gender; mothers**

Historically, in many areas of research regarding child development, the focus has tended to be on *mothers* to the unfortunate exclusion of fathers (and of other potential primary carers). In a large study regarding infant attachment, published in 1997, and in a follow-up paper, van IJzendoorn and De Wolff noted that

> In our meta-analysis on the association between sensitivity and attachment, fathers are conspicuously absent (and) the dearth of studies on the role of the father in infants' development of attachment should unfortunately be considered a matter of fact instead of an opinion. (1997, p. 604)

In addition, many studies have tended to overlook the experience of children and primary carers from 'non-traditional' families, including the children of divorced parents, and blended or stepfamilies. Many studies also appear to be heteronormative in their approach. This situation may have arisen in part because of the different socio-contextual framing that surrounds fathers and 'fatherhood' when compared with mothers and 'motherhood'. In other words, it may be the case that we find strong cultural and social pressures on mothers to conform to certain maternal stereotypes, such as the display of 'nurturing behaviour' towards their children, with a set of different, but equally strong, cultural and social pressures on fathers to behave in often quite different ways. This tends to be the case regardless of the particular culture or society being discussed, although clearly it does not apply universally. Attachment theory is no more able to stand outside these kinds of cultural and social milieux than any other theory of human development. Indeed, one can see in the early writings of *Bowlby* that many of the references we would now conceive of as being relevant to any primary carer (or attachment figure) are written about as though they apply only to mothers. Fortunately, Bowlby later realized his error and wrote explicitly about the importance of mothers and fathers (and of other primary carers too). Such realizations, allied with changing social and cultural norms regarding fatherhood, have led to an increase in the volume of attachment research undertaken with fathers (Bretherton, 2011).

What this research has tended to find is that, although children are just as likely to form attachments with their fathers as they are with their mothers, there may nevertheless be qualitative differences, as well as similarities, between them.

As discussed in the section on the *Adult Attachment Interview*, maternal states of mind with regards to attachment are predictive of infant behaviour in the Strange Situation Procedure, so one obvious question is whether paternal states of mind predict the same. Steele, Steele and Fonagy (1996) looked at one aspect of this question and found that the father's Adult Attachment Interview classification could predict how the infant would behave in the Strange Situation Procedure with the father.

Despite this similarity, they also found some significant differences as well. For example, it appears that whilst fathers do have a direct impact on the nature of the child's attachment relationships, they also have a less direct influence via their impact on the mother's 'state of mind' with regards to attachment. Grossmann *et al.* (2002) studied 44 families over 16 years and examined the child's maternal and paternal attachment relationships at various stages from birth to 16 years of age. Over time, it became clear that the way fathers interact with their children – and in particular how sensitively they do so – becomes more and more significant in predicting the child's longer-term representation of attachment. These findings support the idea that a father's interactive behaviour is perhaps more significant for the child's attachment representations than how the child seeks proximity from their father in times of distress, and that whilst the influences of both maternal and paternal attachment relationships are important, they are important in different ways

Equally, as children grow into adolescence, the ways in which boys and girls perceive their maternal and paternal attachment relationships may also show some gender-related differences. There is some data to suggest that as girls grow older, they may tend to rely more on their mothers for attachment-related support whereas boys tend to rely a bit less on their mothers and both males and females tend to rely less on their fathers for attachment-related support. Whilst there are likely to be *cultural differences* in relation to these findings, they do suggest that some substantial changes may start to take place in the nature of attachment relationships between early to later adolescence and this confirms – if such confirmation were required – the need for a very nuanced approach to such research and for the application of such research to practice.

KEY TEXTS

- Bretherton, I. (2011) 'Fathers in Attachment Theory and Research: A Review', *Early Child Development and Care*, 180 (1–2): pp. 9–23
- Grossmann, K., Grossmann, K., Fremmer-Bombik, E., Kindler, H., Scheuerer-Englisch, H. and Zimmermann, P. (2002) 'The Uniqueness of the Child–Father Attachment Relationship: Fathers' Sensitive and Challenging Play as a Pivotal Variable in a 16-Year Longitudinal Study', *Social Development*, 11 (3): pp. 301–337
- Palm, G. (2014) 'Attachment Theory and Fathers: Moving from "Being There" to "Being With"', *Journal of Family Theory and Review*, doi: 10.1111/jftr.12045

fostering and adoption

SEE ALSO **(reactive) attachment disorder; child maltreatment; neglected children**

The attachment-related experiences and relationships of children in foster or adoptive care have typically been of great interest to attachment researchers and to professionals working with these children. In part, this presumably relates to the likelihood of children in foster or adoptive care having experienced some disruption in their attachment relationships with their birth parents and their potential need for forms of special support in order to develop new attachment relationships with their foster or adoptive carers.

Lanyado (2003) has written about the experiences of children placed into foster care who are then subsequently adopted, noting that such children may have experienced 'multiple traumatic losses' or 'caretaking casualties'. In other words, they may have experienced harsh, difficult, maltreating or neglectful environments prior to being placed in foster care and this makes it unlikely they will have developed *secure attachment* relationships. They may then experience a further loss when they are moved from their foster placement into a permanent, adoptive family, and the significance of this loss may be more or less, depending on the length of the foster placement and whether the child was forming or had formed an attachment relationship with a specific foster carer during this time. From this, often difficult, start they will then need to form new attachment relationships with their adoptive carers. However, despite the widespread popularity of attachment theory in the field of fostering and adoption, Barth *et al.* (2005) have argued that because attachment theory is limited in its ability to predict future attachment patterns – which is reinforced by recent discoveries in *genetic influences* – other theoretical perspectives can contribute as much if not more than attachment theory, and thus it may be that an over-reliance on attachment theory in this field is an example of the *misuses of attachment theory* (although in our view, it is right that attachment theory has a central place when working with children and families, of course we agree that other theories, such as social learning theory, systemic theories and motivational interviewing also have much to contribute).

One relatively common hypothesis regarding children who have been adopted is that they are more likely to develop *insecure attachment* relationships and to present *disorganized attachment* behaviour. Van den Dries *et al.* (2009) studied this idea and found a distinct difference between children adopted before the age of 12 months and children adopted later in life. Specifically, the children adopted earlier were no less likely than any other children to develop secure attachment relationships, whereas those adopted later on were more likely to develop insecure attachment or disorganized attachment relationships. This suggests that where children have experienced relatively long periods of *child maltreatment* or where the adoption involves a neglected child, they may 'carry forward' these (past) experiences into their (future) adoptive family. Hodges *et al.* (2003) investigated the attachment representations of children during the first year of their adoptive placements and found that many, but not all of them, showed increasing levels of security and decreasing levels of insecurity over time.

For children in foster care, Stovall-McClough and Dozier (2004) investigated the attachment behaviour of infants during their first two months in a new foster care placement. They also found that infants placed at an earlier age tended to show earlier and more secure attachment behaviour, as did infants placed with 'secure-autonomous' foster carers as coded using the *Adult Attachment Interview*. Another possible factor in the development of secure attachment relationships by children in foster care appears to relate to the motivations of the foster carers. For example, motivations related to a desire to increase the size of their family and concern for the local community may be positively correlated with secure attachment relationships whereas motivations such as fostering in order to express a personal sense of spirituality or to 'replace' a child now grown up may be positively correlated with insecure attachment relationships.

In recent years, there has also been a growing trend to educate adoptive and foster carers about attachment theory and about attachment disorders in particular. Whilst some of these attempts are well grounded in the theory and science of attachment, many others are unscientific and potentially damaging. For example, advising adoptive or foster carers to look out for 'symptoms' or 'signs' of *attachment disorder*, such as a child laughing when touched (apparently as an indication of physical aversion) or a failure to show 'proper remorse' after behaving badly, are seriously misguided and may make it more likely for such carers to misunderstand the child's behaviour. Fortunately, there are lots of positive examples as well, such as the Attachment and Biobehavioural Catch-up (ABC) intervention, which aims to help foster carers (and adoptive carers) to re-interpret the child's 'alienating' behaviours, to manage any attachment experiences of their own that may be interfering with their ability to care for the child in a nurturing way, and to help the child develop their own internal regulatory mechanisms, for example *emotion (or 'affect') regulation*. Another positive example is group-based parent training, such as the 'Incredible Years Parenting Training Programme' or the 'Triple P – Positive Parenting Programme' – both of which are based largely on social learning theory. As described by Golding (2007), a large body of research exists regarding the efficacy of these kinds of interventions and there appears to be ample scope for incorporating aspects of attachment theory into these existing interventions in order to make them more specifically applicable to the special needs and circumstances of children in foster and adoptive care.

KEY TEXTS

- Barth, R., Crea, T., John, K., Thoburn, J. and Quinton, D. (2005) 'Beyond Attachment Theory and Therapy: Towards Sensitive and Evidence-based Interventions with Foster and Adoptive Families in Distress', *Child and Family Social Work*, 10 (4): pp. 257–268
- Hodges, J., Steele, M., Hillman, S., Henderson, K. and Kaniuk, J. (2003) 'Changes in Attachment Representations over the First Year of Adoptive Placement: Narratives of Maltreated Children', *Clinical Child Psychology and Psychiatry*, 8 (3): pp. 351–367
- Lanyado, M. (2003) 'The Emotional Tasks of Moving from Fostering to Adoption: Transitions, Attachment, Separation and Loss', *Clinical Child Psychology and Psychiatry*, 8 (3): pp. 337–349
- Van den Dries, L., Juffer, F., van IJzendoorn, M. and Bakermans-Kranenburg, M. (2009) 'Fostering Security? A Meta-analysis of Attachment in Adopted Children', *Children and Youth Services Review*, 31 (3): pp. 410–421

g

gender

SEE ALSO attachment relationships in adulthood; cultural differences; fathers; genetic influences; mothers

Attachment is a universal human phenomenon. Nevertheless, there are some qualitative differences in the ways attachment may be expressed and experienced by different individuals – these differences may relate to factors such as *disability, temperament* or more broadly to *genetic influences* on attachment (although caution is required when attributing attachment-related differences to the influence of individual or even relational characteristics without understanding these as being 'operationalized' within particular social settings and in relation to the adequate or inadequate provision of social and environmental support). Whether there are gender differences in the expression of attachment relationships – or in how they are perceived – is less clear.

Some researchers, such as Del Giudice (2009), have identified gender differences with regards to how likely men and women are to present with a particular form of *insecure attachment*, with women being thought more likely to be categorized as ambivalent-resistant and men more likely to be categorized as avoidant. However, these findings have not been widely replicated and even where they have been, it may be that they relate to *cultural differences* rather than anything biological. For example, a Chinese study did not find significant gender-related differences in insecure attachment categories. In 2003, Schmitt reviewed data from 17,804 people across 62 cultural regions and found only small differences between whether men and women were dismissive of the importance of close attachment relationships. From a review of 10,000 *Adult Attachment Interviews*, van IJzendoorn and Bakermans-Kranenburg found no significant differences between men and women either.

With regards to children and the development of *internal working models*, the way these models are expressed via attachment behaviour may differ depending on the gender of the child. For example, Turner (1991) studied four-year-old children and found that boys with insecure attachment relationships tended to be more aggressive, disruptive, assertive, controlling and attention-seeking than boys of the same age with *secure attachment* relationships. Turner also found that girls of the same age with insecure attachment relationships tend to be more dependent and less assertive and controlling whereas girls and boys with secure attachment relationships did not show any significant differences in their behaviour. Again, the results of individual studies need to be interpreted with some caution and, overall, there is no consensus within the attachment literature that there are significant gender differences in relation to attachment.

KEY TEXTS
- Del Giudice, M. (2009) 'Sex, Attachment, and the Development of Reproductive Strategies', *Behavioral and Brain Sciences*, 32 (1): pp. 1–21
- Schmitt, D. (2003) 'Are Men Universally More Dismissing Than Women? Gender Differences in Romantic Attachment Across 62 Cultural Regions', *Personal Relationships*, 10 (3): pp. 307–331
- Turner, P. (1991) 'Relations between Attachment, Gender, and Behavior with Peers in Preschool', *Child Development*, 62 (6): pp. 1475–1488

genetic influences

SEE ALSO **evolutionary insights; fathers; mothers; temperament**

Attachment theory is predicated on the importance of caregiving and relational experiences for the quality and nature of *internal working models* and on the expression of attachment behaviour across the lifespan. In particular, special attention is given to early caregiving and relational experiences as these are assumed to influence the formation of internal working models whereas later experiences can only influence models that have already formed (albeit, internal working models always remain amenable to change). There is a large body of research to suggest that for infants, the *attunement and sensitivity* of their attachment figure's behaviour is a significant influence on the quality and nature of the child's attachment relationship. However, this focus on experience – on the impact of the environment – should not distract us from the growing body of research regarding genetic influences on attachment. One of the more consistent findings from the *history of attachment theory and research* is that the attachment figure's attunement and sensitivity accounts for less of the variance between different attachment relationships than was perhaps originally envisaged. In other words, how sensitive and attuned (or not) attachment figures are towards the infant does explain a significant amount of the variance in the nature of infant attachment relationships but not as much of the variance as had been anticipated. Another portion of the variance can be explained in relation to environmental factors other than the attachment figure's sensitivity, such as income, family size, the age of the attachment figure and their level of education and the presence of (potentially) stressful life events such as the loss of an attachment figure, the birth of a sibling or severe illness in either the attachment figure or the child. As an aside, it is usually considered that the impact of these types of environmental factors is not directly on the infant's attachment relationships but rather mediated through proximal or distal effects on caregiving behaviour. Nevertheless, even taking these additional factors into account, there still remains a portion of the variance between infant attachment relationships that is unexplained by environmental influences.

One particularly interesting hypothesis is the model of differential susceptibility (see Figure 2), which proposes that children may be genetically more or less sensitive to the influences of their caregiving environments. For example, some children, with particular genotypes, may benefit more from positive caregiving environments but also experience more negative consequences from less positive caregiving environments, whilst other children, with different genotypes, may benefit less and suffer less either way, regardless of the caregiving environment.

Bakermans-Kranenburg and van IJzendoorn (2006) tested this hypothesis and found that the dopamine receptor D4 repeat polymorphism (DRD4-7+) has a moderating effect on the association between maternal insensitivity and externalizing behaviour difficulties in children. Children who experienced more insensitive maternal care and had the DRD4-7+ allele tended to display significantly increased levels of behavioural difficulties when compared

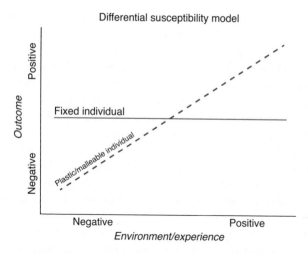

FIGURE 2 *Graphical representation of Belsky's hypothesis of differential susceptibility, with the X-axis representing the quality of the environment and the Y-axis representing outcomes for children*

Source: Public domain image, reproduced from Wikipedia.

to children with the same allele and more sensitive maternal care. Children without the DRD4-7+ allele tended to show no association between levels of maternal sensitivity and externalizing behaviour problems. In other words, children with the DRD4-7+ allele seem to benefit more from sensitive maternal caregiving but experience more difficulties as a result of insensitive maternal caregiving. Children without the DRD4-7+ allele tended to exhibit less behavioural benefits or difficulties either way.[1] This suggests that the differential hypothesis may be valid, at least with regards to some aspects of child development.

Other genes have also been identified as potentially influencing the relationship between the infant's attachment behaviour and the attunement and sensitivity of the attachment figure but because of the complexity of the phenotypes being discussed – attachment and caregiver behaviour – it is clearly not as simple as identifying the 'genes for' attachment. There may be so many genes involved that each one accounts for 1 per cent or less of the variance observed, making the study of these genes and their influences very complex indeed (see Gervai, 2009).

As if this were not complicated enough, we also have the emerging field of epigenetics. Whereas genetics is concerned with (amongst other things) the patterns of inheritance between biologically related carers and their offspring, epigenetics, in broad terms, refers to biological mechanisms and modifications that are not part of the DNA sequence – in other words, to differential gene expression without a preceding change in the underlying DNA. As an example, changing the diet of certain species of mice can affect the expression of certain genes related to fur colour and weight so that two monozygotic (i.e. identical) twin mice may have different coloured fur despite sharing the same DNA at birth. Whilst it is not possible to translate directly from studies of non-human animals to humans, it is not unreasonable to expect that humans experience epigenetic-based differences as well. However, we are far from a complete understanding of the influence of genetics – let alone epigenetics – on attachment, and there is much work to be done in order to develop our understanding of the complex web of relationships between these and other factors. However, what we can say with some confidence is that for young children, environmental factors largely explain the variance in the quality and nature of their attachment relationships, whereas for older children, adolescents and for adults, the degree to which environmental factors retain their significance is less well established.

Only recently Fearon *et al.* (2014) have begun to show how genetic influences on attachment relationships in later childhood and adolescence are probably more important than previously thought. Their research 'included 551 twin pairs aged 15 years recruited from the larger Twins Early Development Study (TEDS). Attachment was assessed using a semistructured interview, the *Child Attachment Interview*' (p. 1038, italics ours, for cross-referencing in this volume). To investigate the relative and proportionate influence of genetic and environmental influences, their sample included identical (MZ) and non-identical (DZ) twin pairs. They found 'robust associations between MZ twins' scores for Coherence and their overall security of attachment … but substantially lower associations for DZ twins … suggesting genetic influence on adolescent attachment …' (p. 1033). The authors went on to add that,

> The results of this study were strikingly different to those that have previously been obtained using twin methodology in

samples of infants and toddlers ... These earlier studies had indicated with considerable consistency that attachment in early life is strongly, if not exclusively, influenced by the environment. Furthermore, they pointed to the important role of the shared environment, in a manner that was highly consistent with predictions from attachment theory. In this study, using a relatively large sample of adolescent twins strong evidence of genetic influence on attachment was found, and estimates of shared environment were effectively at zero. The estimates of heritability we obtained for the scale representing narrative Coherence and the overall 2-way attachment classification (secure vs. insecure) were around 38% and 35% respectively, with the remaining variance being attributable to nonshared environment and measurement error. (Fearon *et al.*, 2014, p. 1037–8)

The authors do point out, however, that the preoccupied attachment pattern (or *ambivalent-resistant attachment*) as well as *disorganized attachment* behaviour were virtually unrepresented in their sample.

At first reading these results appear to challenge a central tenet of attachment theory, namely that *parenting* and environmental factors – 'nurture' – override genetic influences – 'nature'. Certainly this is still true in the early years, during which time hereditary and genetic factors appear to have almost zero influence. So if the Fearon *et al.* (2014) study proves to be replicable, then what might it mean?

Let us propose a purely hypothetical and speculative attempt to begin to make sense of the implications because, in light of these findings, it might be assumed that as pre-teens approach early adolescence there is little that parents can do to affect the attachment relationship of their sons and daughters (many believe this to be the case anyway!). The first point to bear in mind, of course, is that as the relative influence of genes and environment was found to be around 50:50, parenting will still likely have an effect. However, as children get older the simple fact is that they tend to have more people around them to choose from when they need care, protection and comfort. These alternative sources will include: close friends and 'best mates'; later on, boy/girl friends; teachers and parents of their best friends and so on. Let us assume that some of the key psychosocial components involved in the formation of close relationships, such as the need for affiliation, levels of self-esteem and the need for approval, have a relatively high hereditary component. Let us assume further that, as a young person approaches adolescence, these psychosocial components will start to assume far greater importance when s/he develops non-parent-based attachment relationships. We know this to be the case intuitively, and we can see it for ourselves when a growing teenager struggles more and more with group pressure, conformity, risk-taking and so on. It may be that these psychosocial components are the moderating and mediating mechanisms necessary to explain why many parents begin to feel that they are having less influence on their children's attachment relationships as they journey through adolescence. The implications of such an explanation is that the teenager's carers will need to try that much harder to influence them than they did before. On the other hand, the efforts they put in earlier, to offer a *secure base* and safe haven to their children when they were younger, are likely to pay dividends later on when other influences compete with them and sometimes predominate. As Fearon *et al.* (2014) put it:

> later in development children's genetic propensities begin to systematically evoke changes in the relative insensitivity of care provided by their primary attachment figures, which in turn leads to changes in the children's feelings of security in the parental relationship. (p. 1038)

KEY TEXTS
- Belsky, J. (2009) 'Beyond Diathesis Stress: Differential Susceptibility to Environmental Influences', *Psychological Bulletin*, 135 (6): pp. 885–908
- Fearon, P., Shmueli-Goetz, Y., Viding, E., Fonagy, P. and Plomin, R. (2014) 'Genetic and Environmental Influences on Adolescent Attachment', *Journal of Child Psychology and Psychiatry*, 55 (September): pp. 1033–1041
- Gervai, J. (2009) 'Environmental and Genetic Influences on Early Attachment', *Child and Adolescent Psychiatry and Mental Health*, 3 (25), doi: 10.1186/1753-2000-3-25

NOTE
1. As described elsewhere, in particular in the sections on *mothers* and *fathers*, it is unfortunate that this research has not been undertaken with fathers as well. The risk of presenting findings only in relation to

mothers is that it can give the impression that it is solely maternal care that is important and thus if a child displays externalizing behaviour problems, then it must be because of – or at least relate to – insensitive maternal care. This is highly unlikely to be the case and professionals working with children who display externalizing behaviour problems must of course consider the role of all of the child's attachment figures plus a range of other possible influences, rather than drawing the simple but mistaken conclusion that externalizing behaviour problems occur in children solely – or even significantly – because of insensitive maternal care alone.

goal-oriented behaviour

SEE ALSO **internal working models; proximity-seeking and safe-haven behaviours**

The concept of goal-oriented behaviour (sometimes referred to as goal-oriented or goal-corrected behaviour) is reasonably simple and can be seen in many different animal species, including humans. Goal-directed behaviour is any behaviour performed with a set purpose 'in mind', that is behaviour to achieve a particular goal. Whilst this brief definition may seem to suggest that goal-oriented behaviour is necessarily consciously controlled, this is not always the case. As Bargh and Mosella (2008) have noted, 'there now exists substantial evidence that the unconscious is not identifiably less…complex, controlling, deliberative or action-oriented than its counterpart' (the conscious mind; p. 73). Therefore, the categorization of behaviour as goal-oriented does not necessarily mean that it is consciously oriented. This is an important point, particularly in relation to the concept of *internal working models* and how these influence attachment behaviour. However, despite the 'obvious' importance of goal-oriented behaviour, there is arguably a greater body of research with regards to stimulated behaviour, that is, the study of how humans (and other animals) respond to stimuli (the recent trend for research into how human behaviour can be modified via 'nudges' – relatively minor environmental changes – is situated within this tradition). Whilst this research has furthered our understanding of decision-making, many of our daily decisions appear to be, subjectively at least, based on our goals rather than on environmental stimuli (see De Wit and Dickinson, 2009).

Within the context of attachment theory, the link with goal-oriented behaviour lies in the conception of attachment behaviour as being oriented towards the goal of felt security, the receipt of care or protection from an attachment figure. Of course, attachment behaviour is not the only form of human behaviour that has been conceived of as being goal-oriented. For example, children seem to use goal-orientation when asked to imitate the behaviour of another. In other words, if you ask a young child to imitate the behaviour of an adult, they will tend to copy what they assume to be the intentions of the behaviour rather than robotically copying the behaviour itself. If the behaviour they are asked to imitate is 'washing up' and the adult drops a cup on the floor, the child will not usually copy this dropping-of-the-cup but will seem to know that this was unrelated to the overall intention.[1] This suggests that children are innately rather good at taking the 'intentional stance' (which in turn is one of the key building blocks for *mentalization and reflective function*).

In 1969, Mary Ainsworth, an important colleague of *Bowlby* in the *history of attachment theory and research*, wrote a paper about goal-oriented behaviour in which she compared three different theoretical explanations of the 'infant–mother' relationship (as noted elsewhere, contemporary attachment researchers would now rightly refer to 'infant–primary carer' or 'infant–attachment figure' relationships). The three explanations discussed by Ainsworth were – i) psychoanalytical *object relations theory*, ii) social learning theories of dependency and iii) attachment theory. Essentially, object relations and social learning theory both characterize the infant–attachment figure relationship as being one of dependency, whereby the infant relies upon a small number of adults for their physical and emotional care but over time, gradually becomes more and more independent. Attachment theory presents a different explanation, conceiving of the primary care relationships of children as being characterized not by (physical) dependency but by a special type of psychosocial bond (an attachment relationship) that cannot easily be supplanted and that endures well beyond physical independence and to a large extent beyond emotional independence as well (at least in an immediate sense – humans never really become emotionally independent at any age). In other words, many, if not all, infants prefer to maintain their original attachments relationships across the lifespan, barring significant disruptions or environmental changes, although over time these early attachment relationships may become less vital, especially as relationships with peers and *romantic attachments* become more important. This perspective – viewing the relationships between children and their early attachment figures as enduring and significant beyond the stage of physical dependency – arguably provides a far more satisfying explanation as to why children continue to display attachment behaviour as they develop into middle childhood and beyond, and why they continue to direct and orient these behaviours towards their attachment figures in preference to other adults.

For example, a child staying in hospital may appear quite content to be cared for by the nursing staff and they may seek comfort from the nurses when they need it. However, where possible, they will almost always preferentially display attachment behaviour towards their attachment figures and not towards their temporary carers. Thus, attachment behaviour is not related to environmental stimuli per se but it is goal-oriented towards the attainment of comfort or protection from a particular person or persons (the child's attachment figures).

KEY TEXTS

- Aarts, H. and Elliot, J. (eds) (2012) *Goal-Directed Behaviour* (New York: Psychology Press)
- Ainsworth, M. (1969) 'Object Relations, Dependency, and Attachment: A Theoretical Review of the Infant–Mother Relationship', *Child Development*, 40 (4): pp. 969–1026
- Bargh, J. and Mosella, E. (2008) 'The Unconscious Mind', *Perspectives on Psychological Sciences*, 3 (1): pp. 73–79

NOTE

1. Try this at home at your own risk.

h

Harlow's monkey experiments

SEE ALSO Bowlby; evolutionary insights; history of attachment theory and research

As *Bowlby* was developing his theory of attachment, he became aware of the work of Harry Harlow, an American psychologist whose primary research interest was the effect of social isolation and separation on primates. Working at the University of Wisconsin-Madison in the 1930s, the experiments that Harlow was responsible for strike modern sensibilities as completely unethical. Whilst this is undoubtedly true, the results of these experiments were helpful to Bowlby as he developed his early thinking about attachment and so they remain an important reference point in understanding how the theory was first developed.

The most famous of Harlow's experiments involved macaques, a type of Old World monkey. In the wild, macaques have very complicated social structures and, at least for some macaque varieties, as with humans, their infants are highly dependent on adults when they are born and for some time afterwards as they mature. Harlow wanted to understand what elements of the care provided to the infant macaques by the adults was most important to them and so he set up an experiment. Harlow started by taking a number of baby macaques away from their *mothers* as soon as they were born and placing them into wire cages on their own. Harlow then presented each of them with a surrogate 'adult-figure', made of chicken wire and wood. Harlow gave each of the surrogates a unique face and soon found that the infant macaques expressed a preference for their own surrogate over any of the others (presumably by recognizing their unique facial designs). This confirmed Harlow's hypothesis that the infant macaques formed some kind of special bond with a particular adult and that this led them to show a preference for this one particular adult. In a second experiment,

Harlow presented the infant macaques with two surrogates, one of which was covered in soft cloth and one of which was not. In one version of the experiment, the wire surrogate, the one without a cloth covering, held a bottle of food, whilst the cloth-covered surrogate did not. In the second version of the experiment, it was the cloth-covered surrogate that held the bottle of food, whilst the wire surrogate held nothing. In this second version, the infant macaques spent nearly all of their time either feeding or cuddling with the cloth-covered surrogate and entirely ignored the wire surrogate. However, in the first version of the experiment, where the cloth-covered surrogate held nothing and the wire surrogate held the bottle, the infant macaques would go to the wire figure when hungry, in order to feed, but spent the majority of their time cuddling with the cloth-covered surrogate. Thus, Harlow demonstrated how the bond between the infant macaques and their surrogates (and thus, presumably between infant and adult macaques in the wild as well) was based not on the provision of food but on the provision of (emotional?) comfort. He called this phenomenon 'contact comfort'.

In a number of later experiments, Harlow also demonstrated that the same macaques were able to use their surrogates as a *secure base* from which to explore the wider environment and how in the presence of their particular surrogates (and not just any surrogate), the infant macaques were noticeably less anxious than when the surrogate was absent. The parallels with the behaviour of human infants in the *Strange Situation Procedure* are hard to overlook although, as noted at the time, one must proceed cautiously whenever one is seeking to apply the results of experiments with other animals, even other primates, to the understanding of human behaviour and relationships.

KEY TEXTS

- Harlow, H. and Zimmermann, R. (1959) 'Affectional Responses in the Infant Monkey', *Science*, 130: pp. 421–432
- Seay, B. and Harlow, H. (1965) Maternal Separation in the Rhesus Monkey', *Journal of Nervous and Mental Diseases*, 140 (6): pp. 434–441
- Video – https://www.youtube.com/watch?v=OrNBEhzjg8I (some readers will find these images distressing)

history of attachment theory and research

SEE ALSO **Bowlby; evolutionary insights; Harlow's monkey experiments; object relations theory**

John *Bowlby*, often referred to as the 'father of attachment theory', undertook pioneering research in the 1940s and 1950s, studying in particular the behaviour of children separated from their families, such as those who had to be evacuated to the countryside during the Second World War, children in residential homes and children in hospital (this at a time when family members were overtly discouraged from staying with). Bowlby was concerned that the behaviour he observed was not explicable by reference to popular theories of the day, such as the 'secondary-drive' theory, which suggested that children would, over time, form relationships and feel comforted by the presence of any adult who was able to meet their primary needs (for food, water, warmth and so on.). As Bowlby noted, not only did this theory seem inadequate to explain the behaviour he observed, the same theory had arguably been demonstrated as inadequate some years earlier in *Harlow's monkey experiments*.

Instead, Bowlby's observations, combined with the knowledge he synthesized from a range of other research traditions, including *object relations theory* and *evolutionary insights*, led him to develop the hypothesis that there was something special and enduring about the relationships formed between infants and their primary carers and that substitute carers were insufficient from the child's point of view to fulfil this role, even if they provided excellent physical care. Bowlby named this special bond an 'attachment'. Mary Ainsworth, an exceptional researcher who would go on to collaborate with Bowlby for many years, joined him in his work in the early 1950s, and contributed significantly to the development of attachment theory, not least via her contribution to the development of the *Strange Situation Procedure*.

Using the Strange Situation Procedure, Ainsworth and colleagues identified the three organized categories of infant attachment, labelled *ambivalent-resistant attachment, avoidant attachment* and *secure attachment* (see Ainsworth *et al.*, 1978). Ainsworth and her colleagues also found that a significant minority of the children they studied via the Strange Situation Procedure were 'unclassifiable' using these categories and in the late 1980s, Mary Main and Judith

Solomon studied the behaviour of these children in more detail and by so doing, began to codify what became known as *disorganized attachment* behaviour. The use of the Strange Situation Procedure also helped researchers to understand the ways in which children use their attachment figures as a *secure base* from which to explore, about the display of *separation protest* when infants and young children are separated from their attachment figures, and how children use *proximity-seeking and safe-haven behaviours* in order to get closer to their attachment figures during times of heightened anxiety. Later research into the initial development of attachment relationships has discovered that most infants tend to establish a first attachment bond to an attachment figure around the age of six to eight months, although the process of forming this bond is thought to start some months before. Unfortunately, it is the case that many – if not all – early attachment researchers seemed to assume that most attachment figures would be *mothers*, to the exclusion of other potential attachment figures, such as *fathers*, although it is also the case that research regarding fathers as (potential) attachment figures had begun even before Bowlby published the first of his landmark trilogy on attachment theory in 1969. Later attachment researchers did begin to remedy this situation, for example, completing Strange Situation Procedure studies with fathers, grandparents, older siblings and with the carers of children in *fostering and adoption* placements although it is still unfortunately accurate to say that the majority of attachment research is undertaken with mothers.

This early focus on mothers has led to the misguided impression in some quarters that attachment theory is essentially 'about' mothers, to the exclusion of other adults who may function as attachment figures. Another misguided impression is that attachment theory somehow 'supports' the nuclear family (one mother, one father and their biological children) as the optimum caregiving environment for children, with other kinds of families, including blended families, adoptive families, multi-generational families, single carer families and single sex families (including those with LGBT parents), being viewed as somewhat 'deficient' in comparison. Both of these impressions are not only wrong but empirically unsupported given the ample evidence to confirm that children can flourish in a whole variety of caregiving environments (and we know that the majority of children do not live in nuclear families, hence the majority of children who flourish must do so 'despite' living in a different kind of family).

Returning to the history of attachment theory, from Bowlby and Ainsworth's original work, a second strand of research emerged, alongside the work of Main and her colleagues. This second strand is most closely associated with Crittenden, a developmental psychologist, who has proposed a different model for the understanding of attachment. However, although *Crittenden's Dynamic-Maturational Model* is different from the Ainsworth–Main model, it is important to understand how closely Crittenden worked with Bowlby and with Ainsworth in particular and thus, the two models share many similarities along with some crucial conceptual differences. In other words, one should not think of the two models as being essentially the same – they are not – but neither should one consider them to be entirely different either. Where Crittenden's model differs is in its conceptions of the strategic and protective aspects of attachment. For example, Crittenden's model does not include disorganized attachment and considers the behaviour of even *neglected children* and those who have experienced *child maltreatment* to be adaptive to their caregiving environments. These differences have also led to the development of a series of modified *measures of attachment*.

As the research base regarding childhood attachment developed, so interest grew in how attachment theory might be applied to adults. In large part, this exploration of *adult attachment* was enabled by the development, in 1984, of the *Adult Attachment Interview*. Researchers such as Bartholomew and Horowitz helped to link the infant attachment categories identified by Ainsworth, Main and others with attachment 'states of mind' in adults. In addition to this, in the late 1980s, interest began to grow in *romantic attachments*. For example, researchers such as Hazan and Shaver helped to identify how the adult attachment categories of fearful-avoidant and dismissing-avoidant were both linked with the infant category of avoidant attachment, with the former characterized in adulthood by a lack of trust in partners and the latter characterized by a dismissal of the need for emotional closeness. This interest in adult attachment also led to the development of various hypotheses to explain the *trans-generational transmission* of attachment from adult to child.

In order to gather the necessary empirical data against which to test these new theoretical ideas, as well as to gather further data regarding the attachment relationships of children in middle childhood and in adolescence, further measures of attachment were developed including the *Child Attachment Interview* and methods based on *Story Stem Completion. Self-report measures of attachment* were also developed for use with adults, albeit from a quite different research tradition, including the Experiences in Close Relationships-Revised (ECR-R) questionnaire and the Adult Attachment Scale (both of which are freely available online).

KEY TEXTS

- Ainsworth, M. D. S., Blehar, M. C., Waters, E. and Wall, S. (1978) *Patterns of Attachment: A Psychological Study of the Strange Situation* (Hillsdale, NJ: Erlbaum)
- Bretherton, I. (1985) 'Attachment Theory: Retrospect and Prospect', *Monographs of the Society for Research in Child Development*, 50 (1/2): pp. 3–35
- Bretherton, I. (1992) 'The Origins of Attachment Theory: John Bowlby and Mary Ainsworth', *Developmental Psychology*, 28 (5): pp. 759–775

i

insecure attachment

SEE ALSO ambivalent-resistant attachment; avoidant attachment; disorganized attachment; secure attachment

Most children develop a *secure attachment* relationship with their attachment figure(s) but the fact that a significant minority develop insecure attachment relationships was one of the key early findings in the *history of attachment theory and research*. Using the *Strange Situation Procedure*, researchers discovered that insecure attachment could take one of two primary forms – *ambivalent-resistant attachment* or *avoidant attachment*. These two types of attachment, whilst different in some significant ways, also share one crucial similarity – they both indicate that the child will experience a sense of anxiety about the availability of their attachment figure and, hence, that the child finds it difficult to achieve 'felt security' with them. Later researchers would go on to describe an additional element of more extreme examples of insecure attachment known as *disorganized attachment*. The primary difference between disorganized attachment behaviour and ambivalent-resistant attachment and avoidant attachment is that for the latter they indicate that, despite the attachment figure's behaviour being insufficiently sensitive to enable the child to form a secure attachment with them, it is at least predictable or predictably unpredictable enough (for enough of the time) to enable the child to organize his or her own behavioural response. This in turn ensures that the attachment figure will not (often) reject the child outright and that the child will therefore receive at least some level of comfort and protection when required. By contrast, disorganized attachment behaviour suggests that at times, the behaviour of the child's attachment figure is frightening to the child.

Returning to the original research using the Strange Situation Procedure, researchers initially described the two organized forms of insecure attachment as 'anxious-avoidant attachment' or 'anxious-ambivalent-resistant attachment' (rather than more simply ambivalent-resistant attachment and avoidant attachment). The word 'anxiety' is now commonly omitted from many attachment articles and books (as in this one) and whilst this is presumably for reasons of readability, it arguably obscures the core experience of anxiety within the development and maintenance of insecure attachment relationships. In other words, children (and adults) with organized forms of insecure attachment relationships will almost routinely experience a degree of anxiety as to whether their attachment figures will be available for them during times when they need comfort and protection. This applies equally to children with avoidant attachment relationships, as well as those with ambivalent-resistant attachment relationships, even though the behaviour of the former may seem to indicate a lack of concern rather than heightened anxiety (e.g. even in infancy, such children will tend not to approach the attachment figure for comfort after a period of separation). However, as described in the section on avoidant attachment, when such infants are monitored for signs of physiological distress during the Strange Situation Procedure, they tend to show increased palpitation and perspiration during periods of separation and reunion, both of which are common physical signs of increased anxiety.

Further research has helped to elucidate how this anxiety is individually experienced, indicating that whilst children (and adults) with secure attachment relationships or states of mind tend to have a positive self-image and positive expectations of others, in contrast, children (and adults) with avoidant attachment or 'ambivalent-resistant' relationships or states of mind tend to have either a positive self-image or positive expectations of others, but not both. So children with an avoidant attachment relationship tend to have a negative self-image, seeing themselves as perhaps less 'worthy' whilst having sometimes unrealistically positive expectations of others. Such children tend to feel that the responsibility for receiving (or not receiving) care from the attachment figure lies with them, rather than with the adult; that it relies on them being 'worth' caring for. On the other hand, children with ambivalent-resistant attachment relationships develop a more positive self-image but they tend to have negative expectations of others; that whilst they are 'worth' caring for, their attachment figure 'falls short' in some way and is unable to provide the care they need on a consistent basis. Studies with adults have helped to develop the understanding of these experiences of anxiety still further, helped in part by the greater capacity most adults have to use *self-report measures of attachment* and to complete more complex measures of attachment generally. Adults with a preoccupied state of mind with regards to attachment (many of whom will have had ambivalent-resistant attachment relationships in childhood) tend to report having diffi-culty in feeling 'truly close' to other people, including in situations of *romantic attachment*. These adults also tend to report investing a great amount of time in emotional and social intimacy and they may worry that their romantic partner(s) do not really love them. Adults with a dismissive state of mind with regards to attachment (many of whom will have had avoidant attachment relationships in childhood) will also tend to report having difficulty in feeling 'truly close' with others but in contrast with preoccupied adults, they may invest only a little of their time in emotional and social intimacy. In addition, they may report finding it hard to explain how they really feel and to share these feelings with others. As with infant insecure attachment, the common theme between the dismissive and preoc-cupied categories of *adult attachment* appears to be a level of anxiety about whether the individual is loveable or even likeable and there-fore intimacy is something to be concerned about, either because it may not be reciprocated (in the case of preoccupied adults) or because it may lead to discomfort (in the case of dismissive adults). From a professional perspective, this can make it difficult to provide help to adults with insecure states of mind, as they may find it diffi-cult to accept that they need help (especially where the adult has a dismissing state of mind) or that anyone is truly capable of – or even interested in – helping them (especially where the adult has a preoccupied state of mind).

KEY TEXTS

- Byng-Hall, J. (2002) 'Relieving Parentified Children's Burdens in Families with Insecure Attachment Patterns', *Family Process*, 41 (3): pp. 375–388
- Milyavskaya, M. and Lyndon, J. (2013) Strong but Insecure: Examining the Prevalence and Correlates of Insecure Attachment Bonds with

Attachment Figures', *Journal of Social and Personal Relationships*, 30 (5): pp. 529–544
• van IJzendoorn, M., Juffer, F. and Duyvesteyn, M. (1995) 'Breaking the Intergenerational Cycle of Insecure Attachment', *Journal of Child Psychology and Psychiatry*, 36 (2): pp. 225–248

internal working models

SEE ALSO **evolutionary insights; goal-oriented behaviour; object relations theory**

As with many significant concepts within contemporary attachment theory, it was *Bowlby* who originally proposed that all infants develop internal working models of attachment, although clearly in doing so, he drew on a number of other ideas, most notably *object relations theory*. Bowlby theorized that infants develop models of what to expect from other people, from relationships and from themselves and that these models develop as a result of the infant's early relational experiences with their attachment figures (most often their *mother* and *father*). Bowlby argued that these models would give the child a set of beliefs and expectations that would influence how they related to other people and how they perceived this relatedness. Drawing on *evolutionary insights*, Bowlby believed that the development of internal working models of relationships could be understood as a survival strategy, enabling infants, children and adults to more effectively plan their own *goal-oriented behaviour* in relation to other people. Thus, from childhood onwards, these internal working models enable the individual to 'internally simulate' possible behavioural strategies, to 'test them out' and therefore evaluate the likely response from other people. They operate as a 'schema', and offer a way of making sense of previous relational experiences to guide future relational experiences. In Bowlby's own words:

Starting, we may suppose, towards the end of his first year, and probably especially actively during his second and third when he acquires the powerful and extraordinary gift of language, a child is busy constructing working models of how the physical world may be expected to behave, how mother and other significant persons may be expected to behave, how he himself may be expected to behave, and how each interacts with the other. Within the framework of these working models he evaluates his situation and makes his plans. And within the framework of the working models of his mother and himself, he evaluates special aspects of his situation and makes his attachment plans. (1969, p. 354)

Bowlby was very clear that the development of internal working models would be based on actual, real-life experiences with attachment figures – in other words, on how the child interacted with his or her attachment figures. These ideas contrasted markedly with the notion that people behave largely based on internal dynamics, such as the Freudian model of the Id, Ego and Superego. Internal working models are seen as relationship-specific, with a child's view of him or herself being dependent on how their attachment figure behaves with them, how the attachment figure responds to the child's (attachment) behaviour and the way in which the attachment figure helps (or not) the child with *emotion (or 'affect') regulation*. Internal working models of attachment are thus thought to depend upon the individual's *memory* of specific events regarding a small number of attachment figures (things that have happened, where and with whom) and on the emotional impressions of those events (of happiness, fear, anger and so on).

A particularly important aspect of internal workings is that they are 'working' models, in the sense of being 'works in progress'. By describing them in this way, Bowlby sought to emphasize the dynamic and developmental nature of the models. In some cases, children (or adults) may change their perceptions of relationships almost entirely (e.g. changing from having *secure attachment* representations to *insecure attachment* representations). Such changes would most likely occur as a result of significant changes in the way attachment figures behaved with and towards the child. For example, Hodges *et al.* (2003) used *Story Stem Completion* techniques with adopted children and found that over the course of one year post-adoption, many of the children demonstrated an increase in positive representations of attachment figures.

However, the plasticity of internal working models is thought to decrease, at least to some degree, as the child grows older. This is in part because of the growing weight of experiences that help to form the models. However, even where the underlying premise of the models does not change – for example, where a child remains 'secure' in their attachment relationships over the entire period of their childhood – revisions of the models are to be expected as the child grows older, as they develop new abilities and as an attachment figure's expectations of the child change. For example, the child may discover that certain attachment behaviours that used to result in a comforting response when they were younger are now 'rejected' by their attachment figure as less acceptable. Nevertheless, as long as this 'rejection' is not unduly insensitive, harsh or hostile – or as long as the child is able relatively quickly to adapt their behaviour, to receive a comforting response – such occasional lapses in *attunement and sensitivity* are unlikely to disturb the child's underlying secure attachment relationship. One particular area of interest for attachment researchers has been how the child might develop internal working models if they have *multiple attachments* of a distinctive kind with two or more attachment figures (Bretherton, 1985). For example, if a child has a secure attachment relationship with his or her father and an insecure attachment relationship with his or her mother, what kind of internal working models will they develop? Will they maintain distinctive internal working models – and if so, how will this affect their self-image and expectations of others – or will they form a coherent internal working model, combining memories of their experiences with both attachment figures? Unfortunately, although this is an interesting and critical question, there has been little progress in addressing it from an empirical basis.

KEY TEXTS

- Bretherton, I. (1985) 'Attachment Theory: Retrospect and Prospect' in I. Bretheron and E. Waters (eds), Growing Points of Attachment Theory and Research', *Monographs of the Society for Research in Child Development*, 50 (1–2): pp. 3–38
- Bretherton, I. and Munholland, K. (2008) 'Internal Working Models in Attachment Relationships: Elaborating a Central Construct in Attachment Theory' in J. Cassidy and P. Shaver (eds), *Handbook of Attachment: Theory, Research and Clinical Applications*. 2nd edn (New York: Guilford Press): pp. 102–127

interventions

SEE ALSO **fostering and adoption; Video-based Intervention to Promote Positive Parenting**

One of the recurring questions for attachment theory has been how this growing body of knowledge might be used to inform practical or clinical interventions in order to help children and adults who may have experienced attachment-related difficulties. Certainly in the initial stages of the *history of attachment theory and research*, *Bowlby* and others focused more on researching the terrain and territory of attachment theory rather more so than on its potential use in practical settings. However, in the last three to four decades there has been an increasing interest in the application of attachment theory in practice and as a result, there are now several significant and well-evidenced examples of how attachment theory may be used as the basis for interventions with individuals, families and groups. Three of these are briefly discussed in this section – the Circle of Security, Attachment and Biobehavioural Catch-up and Dyadic Developmental Psychotherapy (DDP). In addition, reference is made to some important *misuses of attachment theory* as well.

The 'Circle of Security' model, derived from a combination of attachment theory and *object relations theory*, is a relationship-based intervention with the aim of changing the child's behaviour via modification of the attachment figure's behaviour. Similar in some ways to *Video-based Intervention to Promote Positive Parenting (VIPP)*, using the Circle of Security involves video-taping child–attachment figure interactions (including in the *Strange Situation Procedure*) and reviewing these with the attachment figure in order to increase their *attunement and sensitivity* to their child's cues and increase their abilities of *mentalization and reflective function*. The 'circle' element derives from the idea of an attachment figure as both a *secure base* and as the focus of the child's *proximity-seeking and safe-haven behaviours* – that is, that the attachment figure needs to fulfil the dual role of promoting the child's *exploration and security* and providing them with care and protection. Children with *avoidant attachment* relationships are considered to be less able to use their attachment figures as a safe haven to return to and therefore, they may act as if they want to explore or otherwise maintain some distance from the attachment figure even when they feel anxious. Children with *ambivalent-resistant attachment* relationships are considered to be less able to use their attachment figure as a secure base and therefore, they may act as if they need comfort and protection even when they do not or they may find it difficult to accept the comfort and protection offered by the attachment figure. This in turn may inhibit the child's ability to play and explore. Children who display *disorganized attachment* behaviour are considered to experience fear of their attachment figure and thus to experience a dilemma as to whether the attachment figure is a source of comfort or a source of threat. Recent research has suggested that the Circle of Security model is effective in reducing the occurrence of *insecure attachment* when used with 'high risk' families (Cassidy *et al.*, 2011). VIPP also continues to produce good results. The difference between the two approaches is that VIPP does not assume that the adult needs to understand fully their own early childhood experiences of being parented in order to change the ways they parent their own child/ren.

The Attachment and Biobehavioural Catch-up (ABC) intervention, developed by Mary Dozier, a child development psychologist, is aimed at helping young children aged between six months and two years to develop organized, preferably secure attachment relationships, especially those who have experienced *child maltreatment* or other kinds of disrupted care. The ABC intervention recognizes that such children may find it difficult to accept care and attention from their attachment figures and that this difficulty may be experienced by the attachment figure as a rejection. This perception in turn will tend to make it more difficult for the attachment figure to respond with attunement and sensitivity and thus potentially reinforce the child's difficulty in accepting care and attention. In order to help the child's attachment figure, sessions are provided over a ten-week period and with the help of a trained coach or mentor, the child's attachment figure is provided with 'live feedback' on their behaviour and the behaviour of the child. The aim is to develop the attachment figure's ability to provide nurturing care to the child, even when the child does not elicit such care and when the child actively rejects the attachment figure. The ABC intervention has been shown to be effective for children in *fostering and adoption* placements and for children living with their birth parents. For example, children at risk of maltreatment who participated in the

ABC intervention whilst still living at home showed lower rates of disorganized attachment behaviour than children in a control group (see Bernard *et al.*, 2012).

The third example of a positive attachment-based intervention is Dyadic Developmental Psychotherapy (DDP), used primarily with children in 'fostering and adoption' placements although arguably applicable to children living with their birth parents as well. Developed by Dan Hughes, a clinical psychologist, DDP aims to help foster and adoptive parents care for maltreated children (and *neglected children*) in a particular way, based on the PACE approach to *parenting* – Playfulness, Acceptance, Curiosity and Empathy. PACE is described as a way of thinking, feeling, communicating and behaving with the aim of helping the child to feel secure within their attachment relationships. The approach of DDP can also provide an overall framework for the provision of therapy with children more generally. Despite the clear links between DDP and the principles of attachment theory, it is reasonable to say that the evidence base for the effectiveness of DDP is less well developed than for the Circle of Security or ABC interventions (see Golding, 2014).

As well as these and other positive and evidence-based applications of attachment theory in practice, a number of controversial interventions have been developed as well, many of which have only very dubious links to the supposed underlying theory of attachment. One of the more infamous of these is referred to as 'attachment therapy' or alternatively 'holding therapy', 're-birthing' or even 'Coercive Restraint Therapy'. Before describing this form of 'therapy' in some more detail, it is necessary to be absolutely clear at the outset that we do not believe there is any basis for this type of intervention in attachment theory and we absolutely do not recommend anyone use it (indeed, we strongly recommend you do not use it). We would also highlight that 'holding therapy' has been implicated in some very abusive practices and even tragedies. Having stated our opposition to this kind of intervention as strongly as possible, it is nevertheless worth being informed about it if only on the basis that knowledge is better than a lack of knowledge. The supposed aim of this 'therapy' is to enable previously abused or neglected children who have been removed from the care of their birth parents to develop a new attachment with his or her alternative carers. It often literally involves the child being held or lain upon by the new carer or a therapist in order to prompt responses in the child of rage and despair. This is supposed to produce a type of catharsis in the child, superficially similar to the final stage of grief, as conceptualized by Bowlby, in which the child (in this case) comes to accept that their attachment to their abusive or neglectful birth parent is no more, thus enabling the child to form new attachment relationships. This stage, of holding or laying on the child, may be followed by 're-parenting' behaviours, such as close cuddling, bottle-feeding and lots of eye contact in the belief that this regression to infancy will hasten the child's attachment to his or her new carer(s).

KEY TEXTS

- Bernard, K., Dozier, M., Bick, J., Lewis-Morrarty, E., Lindhiem, O. and Carlson, E. (2012) 'Enhancing Attachment Organization among Maltreated Children: Results of a Randomized Clinical Trial', *Child Development*, 83 (2): pp. 623–636
- Cassidy, J., Woodhouse, S., Sherman, L., Stupica, B. and Lejuez, C. (2011) 'Enhancing Infant Attachment Security: An Examination of Treatment Efficacy and Differential Susceptibility', *Journal of Development and Psychopathology*, 23 (1): pp. 131–148
- Golding, K. (2014) 'Fostering Attachment Group Summary of Research'. Available at http://ddpnetwork.org/backend/wp-content/uploads/2014/01/Fostering-Attachment-Group-Summary-of-Research.Kim-Golding-.pdf

k

kinship care

SEE ALSO **fostering and adoption**

Kinship care – also known as 'friends and family care' – usually refers to formal or informal situations in which children are cared for by someone other than their birth parents, most often (but not always) a member of their wider family. This may include situations when the child has been removed from the care of his or her birth parents with a court order. As these situations usually involve a child moving from the care of their birth parent/s into the care of adults who may or may not be related to the child and who may or may not have had a significant involvement with the child prior to the move, this raises axiomatically questions as to the potential effect on the child's attachment relationships and the expression of their attachment needs. Having said this, there is evidence to suggest that kinship care placements for children are less likely to breakdown than foster care placements (Chamberlain *et al.*, 2006) although whether this is related to attachment per se or perhaps to a greater resilience on the part of kinship carers or to other factors entirely is unclear.

Private fostering may also be considered as a form of kinship care in which the arrangement is informal and where the carer for the child is not a close relative, that is, they are not a step-parent, grandparent, brother, sister, uncle or aunt. Whilst private fostering arrangements have presumably always occurred to one degree or another, it was not until 2005 that the government in the United Kingdom started to collect statistics on the numbers of children in private fostering arrangements. Thus, research into the attachment needs and relationships of privately fostered children has not attracted a great deal of specific attention. Nevertheless, it is of course reasonable to assume that children in private fostering arrangements have similar attachment-related needs to those of other children, although perhaps they may also have additional needs similar to other 'looked after' children. A study conducted by Shaw and colleagues (2010) on behalf of the Department for Children, Schools and Families, noted that in some cases, because private fostering is an informal arrangement, the child probably already knew their carers prior to coming to live with them and this might help the child feel more settled more quickly. Other children in private fostering arrangements may develop emotional problems as a result of the prolonged separation from their birth family. However, as Shaw and colleagues acknowledged in the study, there is only limited data available regarding this group of children and thus it is difficult to draw any conclusions about their needs.

KEY TEXTS

- Chamberlain, P., Price, J., Reid, J., Landsverk, J., Fisher, P. and Stoolmiller, M. (2006) 'Who Disrupts from Placement in Foster and Kinship Care? *Child Abuse and Neglect*, 30 (4): pp. 409–424
- Shaw, C., Brodie, I., Ellis, A., Graham, B., Mainey, A., de Sousa, S. and Willmott, N. (2010) *Research into Private Fostering* (London: Department for Children, Schools and Families)
- Tarren-Sweeney, M. (2013) 'An Investigation of Complex Attachment- and Trauma-related Symptomology among Children in Foster and Kinship Care', *Child Psychiatry and Human Development*, 44 (6): pp. 727–741

1

later life attachments

SEE ALSO **adult attachment; romantic attachments**

Bowlby wrote that attachment characterizes human relationships from 'the cradle to the grave' and he speculated that during later life, attachment relationships might form between members of the older generation and members of young generations, reversing some of the dynamics in early life. In other words, older people may form attachment relationships with their adult children (as well as maintaining attachment relationships they have already, such as *romantic attachments* with partners). However, despite Bowlby's interest in later life attachment, the majority of attachment research in the past 50 years or so has tended to focus on childhood more so than on *adult attachment*. More recently, there has been some growing interest in attachment in later life, not least because of increasing life expectancy in many developed countries (according to the Office for National Statistics, life expectancy at birth in the United Kingdom in 1951 was around 65 for males and 70 for females; by 2012, these estimates had increased to around 79 and 83 respectively). Such research has tended to support the idea that attachment security is a key feature of close relationships across the lifespan, from infancy through to later life, although questions as to the long-term stability of attachment patterns remain open due to a lack of empirical, longitudinal data. In relation to later life attachment, one area of interest is how the process of ageing might affect attachment (see Shemmings, 2006). After all, there are thought to be age-related differences in personality, as well as age-related differences in social norms, roles and relationships.

Chopik, Edelstein and Fraley (2013) sought to investigate attachment in later life by collecting data from 86,555 people aged between 18 and 70 using the Experiences in Close Relationships-Revised (ECR-R) questionnaire (see *self-report measures of attachment*). This questionnaire aims to assess individual differences in attachment-related anxiety and avoidance, including an individual's comfort with closeness, and concern about being abandoned. Broadly speaking, this research found that anxiety was highest in young adulthood (18–22 years) when compared with early adulthood (23–29 years), middle adulthood (30–49 years) and later adulthood (50–70 years). Avoidance, however, was lower in young adulthood, higher in middle adulthood and slightly lower again in older adulthood. Considering the impact of relationship-status, it appeared that anxiety was generally higher amongst single people than those in a romantic relationship, and with regards to *gender*, anxiety was generally higher for women than men, especially in young adult-hood. For avoidance, the pattern was similar again, with single people reporting higher levels of avoidance and single females demonstrating particularly high levels. Despite these differences, the researchers noted that one of their more notable findings was how similar men and women are across the lifespan with regards to attachment-related anxiety and avoidance. The clearest differences they found related to relationship-status but with some effects seemingly related to the process of ageing itself. Whilst such data cannot identify causal connections, it may be that the development of longer-standing, close relationships helps to reduce attachment-related feelings of anxiety and avoidance, or it may be that individuals with *secure attachment* patterns or states of mind are more likely to form longer-standing, close relationships.

With regards to the increasingly common and age-related syndrome (or group of syndromes) of dementia, in which people may experience memory loss, a decrease in their mental agility and increasing difficulties in language, understanding and judgement, attachment theory may help to elucidate the subjective experience of individuals with dementia. In part, this potential is highlighted by the shift away from a purely medical model of dementia towards a more social, person-centred approach (albeit such progress is patchy and incomplete). For example, attachment theory may help us to understand why some people with dementia become very concerned about seeing their parents, despite the fact that for many people with dementia, they are of an age where their birth parents are likely deceased. For some adults with dementia, they may display what might otherwise be referred to as attachment behaviour, such as calling out for their parents, searching for them and asking to be allowed to return to their childhood home. The conception of this behaviour as being attachment-related has informed some possible treatments for people with dementia such as 'stimulated presence therapy', in which the person is given an audio recording of a family member speaking. 'Doll therapy' may also help to meet the attachment-related needs of people with dementia, with the provision of a doll seeming to induce, for some, positive recollections of child–parent relationships from the past. Thus, although this is a very new and developing area of research, attachment theory may provide a useful framework for understanding some of the experiences and some aspects of the behaviour of people with dementia. New developments in virtual technology, pioneered by a team headed by the University of Kent in the United Kingdom, has produced a prototype avatar – RITA (Responsive, InTeractive Avatar) – for older people, based upon the principles of attachment theory and research (see http://rita.me.uk/demo/).

KEY TEXTS

- Browne, C. and Shlosberg, E. (2006) 'Attachment Theory, Ageing and Dementia: A Review of the Literature', *Aging and Mental Health*, 10 (2): pp. 134–142
- Chopik, W., Edelstein, R. and Fraley, R. (2013) 'From the Cradle to the Grave: Age Differences in Attachment from Early Adulthood to Old Age', *Journal of Personality*, 81 (2): pp. 171–183
- Shemmings, D. (2006) Using Adult Attachment Theory to Differentiate Adult Children's Internal Working Models of Later Life Filial Relationships', *Journal of Aging Studies*, 20 (2): pp. 177–191

loss and bereavement

SEE ALSO **adult attachment; unresolved loss and trauma**

Bowlby wrote extensively on the significance of loss and bereavement in the context of attachment relationships. He showed how loss and bereavement could shape a person's state of mind with regards to attachment but also how a person's previous experience of attachment relationships influenced their response to loss and bereavement. Bowlby's key insight was to observe the similarity between the behaviour of children experiencing prolonged separation from an attachment figure and the response of both children and adults to the permanent loss of an attachment figure (behaviour more commonly associated with mourning). Children who experience a prolonged separation will typically express a sense of heightened anxiety and, over time, of panic, frustration and anger. These feelings may be directed both inwardly and outwardly towards the absent attachment figure. Some children in this situation may search for the missing attachment figure and have great difficulty in accepting that they are really absent. Other children may maintain a more passive vigil, seemingly watching for the return of the missing attachment figure. Over time, most children tend to stop this kind of behaviour and become more introverted, apparently resigning themselves to the attachment figure's absence. Some children even remain in this state of relative stillness even after their attachment figure returns, as if having 'adjusted' to the absence, they are now having difficulty in accepting that they have returned.

Bowlby's perception of the similarity between this behaviour and the process commonly known as mourning led to a theoretical conception of attachment, separation and loss (and bereavement) being intimately related. Without attachment, there would arguably be a less intense sense of loss when a loved one dies. As Sir Richard Bowlby, John Bowlby's son, has written:

> The first time the full significance of [my father's] work struck me was [when] he said to me, 'You know how distressed small children get if they're lost and can't find their mother and how they keep searching'? Well, I suspect it's the same feeling that adults have when a loved one dies, they keep on searching too. I think it's the same instinct that starts in infancy and evolves throughout life as people grow up. (Bowlby, 2005, pp. vi–vii, cited in Shaver and Fraley, 2006)

Together with Colin Murray Parkes, John Bowlby went on to outline a four-stage model of grief, proposing that the first stage is characterized by a sense of numbness and shock, essentially a denial of what has occurred. The second stage is characterized by an apparent realization of the loss and is typically accompanied by crying, anxiety, tension and for some a loss of interest in the wider world. The third stage then involves a more generalized sense of despair and low mood before a fourth stage of 're-organization', in which the permanence of the loss is 'accepted' and the mourning individual 'lets go' of their previous attachment to the deceased person. Of course, any model of such a complex process as mourning can only ever be a simplification and more recent research, as described by Parkes (2006), has highlighted the many and varied responses to loss and bereavement that different people experience.

More contemporary models of grief have since been developed, many of which, if not all, draw on attachment theory to one extent or another. One example is the Dual Process Model (DPM) of bereavement. First published in 1999, this model seeks to offer a more nuanced understanding of loss and bereavement than John Bowlby's four-stage model and in particular, it challenges the idea that bereaved persons need to focus on their feelings of loss in order to 'work through them' and recover from them. Instead, the DPM proposes there are two main aspects to bereavement, both of which may operate at the same time or at different times – loss-orientation (which may include familiar attachment-related behaviours such as 'searching for the lost person') and restoration-orientation (which may include a reorientation to a world in which the deceased person is now absent). Thus, the DPM seeks to recognize that the grieving process involves not a series of stages but rather an oscillation between various aspects of loss and at other times, an active avoidance of thinking about the loss at all. Therefore, where John Bowlby's approach described a discrete state of protest, the DPM recognizes that people may experience intense feelings of anger and guilt because of their loss but in combination with periods where they think mainly about other things, without these experiences being organized into anything like discrete stages.

In summary, the DPM incorporates important elements of attachment theory but also seeks to recognize that, as Bowlby wrote about in relation to attachment more generally, attachment behaviour is not the only organizing factor in human development and, hence, there is no reason that it should be within the process of grief and mourning in response to loss and bereavement either.

KEY TEXTS

- Bowlby, J. and Parkes, C. M. (1970) Separation and Loss within the Family' in E. J. Anthony (ed.), *The Child in His Family* (New York: J. Wiley)

- Parkes, C. M. (2006) *Love and Loss: The Roots of Grief and Its Complications* (London: Routledge)
- Shaver, P. and Fraley, C. (2008) 'Attachment, Loss and Grief: Bowlby's Views and Current Controversies' in J. Cassidy and P. Shaver (eds), *Handbook of Attachment: Theory, Research and Clinical Implications.* 2nd edn (London: Guilford Press): pp. 48–77

m

measures of attachment

SEE ALSO Adult Attachment Interview; Child Attachment Interview; self-report measures of attachment; Story Stem Completion; Strange Situation Procedure

As attachment theory has grown in popularity, so various measures of attachment have been developed in order to investigate, measure and describe different aspects of attachment in both adults and children. The first systematic measure of attachment – often referred to as the 'gold standard' – is the *Strange Situation Procedure*, devised by Mary Ainsworth and colleagues. Other relatively well-developed measures of attachment include the *Adult Attachment Interview*, *Child Attachment Interview* and *Story Stem Completion* tasks. A suite of *self-report measures of attachment* has also been developed, particularly for use with adults. As these measures are all discussed within their own dedicated sections, this chapter will discuss the nature of attachment measures more broadly.

In general terms, most attachment measures seek to prompt the individual (or the relational dyad) being studied to either display attachment or caregiving behaviour (as in the Strange Situation Procedure) or to 'activate' attachment-related *memory* systems. For young children (infants and toddlers), it is relatively easy to prompt the display of attachment behaviour, for example, by briefly separating them from an attachment figure. Such short separations, often for no longer than four or five minutes, are almost always sufficient to prompt an infant or toddler to display attachment behaviour, including *proximity-seeking and safe-haven behaviours*. Causing an infant or toddler to feel anxious on purpose may raise certain ethical concerns about the use of such a method and so it is important to recall, firstly, that only those with suitable training are able to readily analyse attachment behaviour (and hence, those without suitable training should not attempt to do so) and, secondly, that these kinds of separations will, for many children, be familiar to daily occurrences of separation in their everyday lives (such as when they are left to sit at the dinner table for a couple of minutes whilst their primary carer goes to get something from the kitchen, or when a parent needs to go to the bathroom, or answer the door to a caller).

For older children and adults, it is more difficult to prompt the display of attachment behaviour. For example, for preschool children who attend day care – and even for those who do not – the kind of brief separations used in the Strange Situation Procedure are usually insufficient to induce the display of attachment behaviour and, in any event, beyond infancy the child's ability to use increasingly sophisticated forms of attachment behaviour makes it even more difficult to identify and analyse. Thus, measures of attachment for older children and adults usually aim to prompt the recollection and description of attachment-related events, such as those involving *loss and bereavement*. However, regardless of the particular method, the aim of every measure of attachment is to reveal the respondent's underlying expectations and perceptions; or, put another way, to reveal their *internal working models* of attachment.

One might ask why, if attachment characterizes a significant facet of many close relationships, such formal measures of attachment are needed at all, as opposed to the arguably more straightforward approach of observing people and their interactions ('naturalistic observation'). However, the difficulty with attempting to observe so-called naturally occurring attachment behaviour is that, whilst attachment is an important component of many close relationships, it is not the only component and in much of daily life a person's 'attachment system' is not routinely activated as long as they are not experiencing situations of heightened anxiety. In situations of low or even moderate anxiety, other behavioural or representational systems may be activated in preference to the attachment system. For example, if one were to observe an infant at home in their normal environment, with their mother, father or other primary carers, then over time one would be able to identify the child's display of *separation protest* and the use of the attachment figure as a *secure base* but it has been estimated that one would need to continually observe the infant for around seven hours in order to reliably assess the child's attachment behaviour and to characterize the nature of their attachment relationship (i.e. whether it is a *secure attachment* or *insecure attachment*). Therefore, the purpose of a measure such as the Strange Situation Procedure is to place the child and an attachment figure in a suitably unusual (strange) situation, in order to deliberately provoke the display of attachment behaviour. Other attachment measures also tend to involve an element of 'surprising the unconscious' in order to activate the respondent's attachment system (although not as directly as in the Strange Situation Procedure).

KEY TEXTS

- Griffin, D. and Bartholomew, K. (1994b) 'Models of the Self and Other: Fundamental Dimensions Underlying Measures of Adult Attachment', *Journal of Personality and Social Psychology*, 67 (3): pp. 430–445
- O'Connor, T. and Byrne, J. (2007) 'Attachment Measures for Research and Practice', *Child and Adolescent Mental Health*, 12 (4): pp. 187–192
- Ravitz, P., Maunder, R., Hunter, J., Sthankiya, B. and Lancee, W. (2010) 'Adult Attachment Measures: A 25-Year Review', *Journal of Psychosomatic Research*, 69 (4): pp. 419–432

memory

SEE ALSO **dissociation; internal working models; unresolved loss and trauma**

Understanding *internal working models* and attachment representations often involves the analysis of attachment-related memories, especially when working with adolescents and adults, and there is an argument that attachment theory is a theory of how representations of relational experiences are encoded and recalled within different memory systems. For example, there is evidence to suggest that adults with *avoidant attachment* 'states of mind' tend to have more difficulty recalling emotional experiences within the context of close relationships than adults with more secure states of mind and this appears to relate to adults of the former category encoding less information about these experiences (Fraley, Garner and Shaver, 2000). An adult with an avoidant state of mind will remember less about their emotional experiences because they 'record' less information about them than other adults typically will. However, as with many aspects of contemporary attachment theory, the interaction between different memory systems and attachment is complex.

From a broad psychological perspective, there are thought to be two primary types of memory – explicit and implicit. Explicit memory is perhaps the more familiar of the two and involves the recollection of events, data and facts (What year were you born? Who is the prime minister? Where do you live?). The explicit memory system also includes autobiographical memories. For example, in order to answer the following question (taken from the *Child Attachment Interview*) – 'When you are upset, what do you do?' – one would need to access the explicit memory system.

The implicit memory system is arguably more complex and involves aspects of cognition, perception, emotion, behaviour, physical sensation and mental models, including internal working models of attachment. *Bowlby* noted how in these different systems, memories could be stored both 'semantically', including general propositions about the self ('I am loveable', 'I am not worth caring about'), and 'episodically', which would include specific times when an attachment figure demonstrated caring or rejecting behaviour. Implicit and explicit memories also differ in that when recalling implicit memories, there is often no subjective sense of 'remembering', in the way there is when recalling explicit memories. If you were asked to remember your first day at school, this would rely on your explicit memory system and would probably involve a sensation of remembering, of somehow 'reaching into' your own past in order to provide an answer. However, if you were asked to describe how to ride a bike (or how to swim, run, walk, crawl, etc.), the sensation of 'remembering' tends to feel very different and it may even feel as if the answer (or the question) does not involve remembering at all.

The link with attachment theory is that attachment-related memories tend to be primarily implicit rather than explicit. In other words, early and later experiences with attachment figures are retained through the implicit memory system (in addition to specific examples within the explicit memory system) and create a 'sense of knowing' about close relationships that is quite distinct from the recollection of particular events. This distinction – between explicit and implicit memories – highlights the importance, when thinking about attachment, of focusing not on what people say about their attachment relationships but on the ways in which they talk about attachment experiences and memories and how they behave in relation to their attachment figures. For example, although the *Adult Attachment Interview* asks questions that require explicit memory-based answers, the analysis of the interview is based not on what is said but on how it is said: on the quality and nature of the overall discourse, and on the implicit messages that people have 'taken away from' their specific experiences.

Crittenden's Dynamic-Maturational Model invokes a more complex model of attachment than the one described above, involving eight memory systems – biological (organic states and 'body talk'), cognitive (procedural and semantic), affective (imaged and connotative language) and integrative (episodic and reflective integration). Crittenden argues that it is the combination of memories from these different areas that results in 'dispositional representations' (or internal working models) of attachment.

KEY TEXTS
- Alexander, K., Quas, J. and Goodman, G. (2002) 'Theoretical Advances in Understanding Children's Memory for Distressing Events: The Role of Attachment', *Developmental Review*, 22 (3): pp. 490–519
- Gentzler, A. and Kerns, K. (2006) 'Adult Attachment and Memory of Emotional Reactions to Negative and Positive Events', *Journal of Cognition and Emotion*, 20 (1): pp. 20–42
- Thompson, R. and Madigan, S. (2005) *Memory: The Key to Consciousness* (New Jersey: Princeton University Press)

mentalization and reflective function

SEE ALSO **attunement and sensitivity; trans-generational transmission; zero empathy**

Mentalization refers to the ability to reflect upon one's own state of mind and to reflect upon other people's states of mind, particularly in relation to what they might be feeling and why and how this relates to behaviour. Reflective functioning is the 'operationalization' of mentalization within the context of an attachment relationship. Slade (2005) has described reflective functioning as an 'essential human characteristic', enabling us to 'understand behaviour in light of underlying mental states and intentions' (p. 269). In the context of child–adult relationships, reflective functioning concerns the attachment figure's ability to understand his or her internal mental experiences and those of the child. However, it is not only adults who mentalize about themselves and others – children also develop this ability and crucially, the ways in which the child is mentalized 'about', especially within the context of attachment relationships, appears to correlate with the child's own development of mentalization.

The concept of mentalization was originally developed by a team of psychoanalytically oriented attachment researchers, led by Peter Fonagy, as a way of explaining and understanding the human ability to 'see beyond' behaviour and to understand mental states. Fonagy and colleagues argued that this ability underpins the development of all social relationships (including attachment relationships), enabling us to 'think about feelings' and to 'feel about thinking'. Despite this supposed centrality of mentalization in the development of social relationships, it nevertheless appears that mentalization is something learned rather than something innate. In particular, mentalization usually first develops through relational interactions between the infant and his or her attachment figures. Slade (2005) has described how the attachment figure's ability to 'hold in mind' the child as a unique individual with feelings, desires and intentions, offers the child an opportunity to learn about his or her own internal experiences (mental states) and those of others, from the attachment figure's responses and behaviour.

However, although mentalization abilities are thought to develop over time, this process nevertheless relies on an innate ability (much like birds have an innate ability to fly but nevertheless need to learn and practice in order to become proficient), which has been described by the America philosopher, Daniel Dennett, as the 'intentional stance':

> You decide to treat the object whose behavior is to be predicted as a rational agent; then you figure out what beliefs that agent ought to have, given its place in the world and its purpose. Then you figure out what desires it ought to have, on the same considerations, and finally you predict that this rational agent will act to further its goals in the light of its beliefs. A little practical reasoning from the chosen set of beliefs and desires will in most instances yield a decision about what the agent ought to do; that is what you predict the agent will do. (1996, p. 17)

This ability to predict mental states in others means that behaviour can be understood as meaningful and this enables predictions to be made as to how other people might behave. This suggests a link between mentalization – being able to observe someone's behaviour and predict the underlying mental states – and the development of *internal working models* of attachment. However, 'Individuals differ in the extent to which they can go beyond observable phenomena (behaviour) to explain their own and others' actions in terms of belief, desires, plans, and so on' (Fonagy and Target, 1999, p. 680).

Thus the link between attachment and mentalization is twofold – firstly, it is within the context of attachment relationships that the child develops their mentalization abilities and, secondly, it is mentalization that enables the child to understand and predict the behaviour of their attachment figures (and to develop internal working models of attachment). However, as noted by Fonagy and Target, different individuals will vary in the extent of their abilities to predict the mental states that may underlie someone else's behaviour (and their own) as well as how capable they are of predicting future behaviour based on estimations of current or past mental states. Within this context, a higher facility for 'reflective functioning' (i.e. mentalization within the context of an attachment relationship) refers to the understanding that emotional responses can vary in intensity, that the intensity of emotional reactions can increase and diminish over time, that emotions can be disguised, and that one 'feeling state' can trigger other 'feeling states', both in the self and in others. Most importantly, it involves a recognition that emotions and other mental states are key to understanding and predicting behaviour and thus, an individual with a higher ability of reflective functioning is better able to integrate (internal, unobservable) emotions and intentions with (external, observable) behaviours within their internal working models.

From their early studies of reflective functioning, using the *Adult Attachment Interview*, Fonagy *et al.* (1991) found that many adults had these kinds of 'higher abilities' and were able to demonstrate an understanding of their own parents' behaviour (during their childhood) in terms of emotions and mental states. For example, one of the questions in the Adult Attachment Interview is 'Why do you think your parents behaved the way they did'? Adults with higher capacities for reflective functioning tend to answer this question by reference to the mental states of their parents, perhaps saying something like,

> my mum used to tell me off a lot whenever I was late home. Sometimes she could say really nasty things actually, but now I'm a mum, I think I understand it, although I would never use that kind of language with my own children – but I think she probably did it because she was worried about me and wanted me to be safe.

However, they also found that some adults had less well-developed abilities and tended to make sense of their parents' behaviour based mainly on what they had observed rather than by reference to any possible underlying mental states. Adults in this latter category might answer the same question from the Adult Attachment Interview in quite different ways – for example,

> to be honest, my mum was always telling me off, no matter what I used to do. She used to just shout at me – I remember one time I came home a bit late and she just let rip, calling me every name under the sun. She was horrible to me, really.

The key difference between this answer and the previous one lies in the absence of any references to the mother's mental states that may have underpinned her behaviour. Note that in both examples, there is a recognition on the part of the now grown-up child that the way in which the mother told her off was 'nasty' or 'horrible' but in the former, this behaviour is (at least) explicable by reference to an underlying mental state of being worried and concerned for the child's safety, whereas in the latter, it is just inexplicable, or explicable only in relation to the mother's 'horrible' personal characteristics.

As well as considering how adults are more or less able to make sense of their own parents' behaviour by reference to mental states, reflective functioning can also be useful for thinking about the nature of the relationship between an *adult attachment* figure and their own children. Of course, when considering mentalization or reflective functioning in relation to specific child–adult dyads, it is important to do so by reference to the child's development. For example, it is much easier (for many) to make reasonable guesses as to what a two-year-old child might be thinking and feeling than it is to do the same with a three-month-old child. Nevertheless, as long as the child's development is taken into context, it is possible to start thinking about the mentalization abilities of an attachment figure by reflecting upon how they speak about their child. Attachment figures with less well-developed abilities to mentalize might talk about their child as if they have little or no internal experiences of their own. They may seem to suggest that their child is always 'fine' even when they are crying or are otherwise distressed, or they may focus on the physical or (what they assume to be) enduring personality traits of the child ('he's cute', 'she's just stubborn'). They may also deny or minimize their own experience of what we know are very common feelings for primary carers, such as guilt, anger or joy, especially in relation to their caring role. In situations of child abuse and neglect more significant mentalizing problems are often noted. This can include the attribution of negative intentions to the child – 'she hates me' or 'he can't stand being near me'. It can also include persecutory attributions, which are even more concerning, whereby the carer believes the child is actively trying to upset or anger them or even potentially to harm them. This is particularly worrying if the carer believes their baby or toddler holds such thoughts about them.

The majority of attachment figures are able to recognize that their child does have feelings and thoughts of their own and will tend to comment on these, perhaps saying, 'he's sad' or 'she wants me to play with her' (see Slade, 2005). Many will also make links between their child's internal, mental states and their physical states and external behaviour and this is really the true mark of developed mentalization – 'he's having a tantrum at the moment (behaviour) because he's overtired (physical state) and fed up because I can't play with him right now (mental state)'. Slade (2005) gives the following example of a particularly well-developed and mentalized account of a child's behaviour by her mother:

> Sometimes she gets frustrated and angry in ways that I'm not sure I understand. She points to one thing and I hand it to her, but it turns out that's not really what she wanted. It feels very confusing to me when I'm not sure how she's feeling, especially when she's upset. Sometimes she'll want me to do something

and I won't let her because it's dangerous, and so she'll get angry. I may try to pick her up and she obviously didn't want to be picked up because she's in the middle of being angry and I interrupted her. In those moments it's me who has the need to pick her up and make her feel better, so I'll put her back down. (2005, p. 279)

In this example, the mother is doing several important things – she is recognizing the child's mental states ('frustrated and angry') whilst acknowledging that she has the potential to be wrong about what is really going on for her child ('it turns out that's not really what she wanted'). She links this with her own mental states ('It feels very confusing to me'), recognizes that sometimes she wants different things from the child ('she'll want me to do something and I won't let her') and is curious about how her behaviour impacts on the child's mental states ('and so she'll get angry'). The mother also demonstrates her understanding that, at times, she behaves in response to her own mental states ('it's me who has the need to pick her up') rather than the child's ('she obviously didn't want to be picked up') and this recognition helps her to modify her own behaviour in response ('so I'll put her back down again'). Described in this way, it appears to be a complicated process – and it is – but of course, in 'real life', this all tends to happen dynamically and without a great deal of conscious thought (relying more on implicit rather than explicit *memory*). Analysed in this way, it may become apparent how often and easily most of us mentalize about our own behaviour simultaneously with that of others but equally, as you become more attuned to these kinds of narrative descriptions, you may also start to notice where they are absent.

Significantly, Fonagy and colleagues also found a strong correlation between adults with more developed capacities for reflective functioning, secure/autonomous attachment classifications and children with *secure attachment* relationships. Similarly, they found a correlation between adults with less well-developed abilities of reflective functioning, insecure classifications of those adults and children with *insecure attachment* relationships. That is to say, an attachment figure's ability to understand and reflect upon his or her child's internal world is a reasonably good predictor of whether the child will have or will develop a secure attachment relationship or an insecure attachment relationship with the particular attachment figure. Given the central role of mentalization within attachment relationships, it is unsurprising that, according to Madigan *et al.* (2006), mentalization is probably one of the more significant variables within the *trans-generational transmission* of attachment relationships.

KEY TEXTS

- Dennett, D. (1996) *The Intentional Stance*. 6th edn (Cambridge, MA: MIT Press)
- Fonagy, P. and Target, M. (1996) 'Attachment and Reflective Function: Their Role in Self-organization', *Development and Psychopathology*, 9 (4): pp. 679–700
- Fonagy, P., Bateman, A. and Bateman, A. (2011) 'The Widening Scope of Mentalization: A Discussion', *Psychology and Psychotherapy: Theory, Research and Practice*, 84 (1): pp. 98–110
- Slade, A. (2005) 'Parental Reflective Functioning: An Introduction', *Attachment and Human Development*, 7 (3): pp. 269–281

misuses of attachment theory

SEE ALSO criticisms of attachment theory; interventions

Attachment theory is in many ways a seductively simple theory, and yet in other ways it is deceptively complex. Combined with the popularity of attachment theory among many health and social care professionals, this may explain why it is at times misused. One of the more egregious examples of the misuse of attachment (so-called holding therapy) is discussed in the section on *interventions* but there are other examples too.

One of the more common misuses is in the imprecise use of theoretical terminology, such as when reference is made to 'strong' or 'weak' attachment. Waters and McIntosh (2011) have criticized exactly this kind of imprecision, which they argue often accompanies references to attachment theory. Waters and McIntosh argue, correctly in our view, that this kind of language – 'strong' or 'weak' attachment – has no relevance within contemporary attachment theory. Holland (2010) has studied how social workers assess children and found that they will often make elementary mistakes when referring to a child's attachment behaviour or relationships.

Holland describes one social worker in particular who observed an infant 'clinging to her mother' and who described this behaviour as indicative of a 'strong attachment'. In actual fact, clingy behaviour in a child of this age is more likely to indicate an *insecure attachment* relationship rather than a *secure attachment* although, as Holland rightly notes, in order to draw a meaningful conclusion about the nature of a child's attachment relationship, one must at the very least observe the child on more than one occasion, especially when the observation is in a naturalistic setting (i.e. not based on formal *measures of attachment* such as the *Strange Situation Procedure*).

Another common misuse of attachment theory has been identified by Barth *et al.* (2005) who argued that, despite the popularity of attachment theory within health and social care, the 'scientific base of attachment theory is limited both in terms of its ability to predict future behaviours, and...with regard to its use as the underpinning theory for therapeutic intervention with children experiencing conduct problems' (p. 257). With regards to the predictive power of early attachment-related experiences, Barth and colleagues noted that although attachment has been found to be relatively stable over time, at least in some samples, *internal working models* of attachment are by definition susceptible to change over time and thus they 'lack predictive power when considering the future life chances of the sorts of children needing child welfare services' (p. 258). Because we do not know what experiences or circumstances the child might encounter in future, we cannot make individual predictions based on current attachment representations and relationships even though we know with a relatively high degree of certainty, for example, that children with secure attachment relationships will have better long-term outcomes in a range of areas than children displaying *disorganized attachment* behaviour.

As summarized by Sroufe *et al.* (1999):

Early experience does not cause later pathology in a linear way; yet, it has special significance due to the complex, systemic, transactional nature of development. Prior history is part of current context, playing a role in selection, engagement, and interpretation of subsequent experience and in the use of available environmental supports. Finally, except in very extreme cases, early anxious attachment is not a direct cause of psychopathology but is an initiator of pathways probabilistically associated with later pathology. (p. 1)

Additional criticisms have also been made of the misuse of attachment theory in social policy (as opposed to practice). White and Wastell (unpublished, 2013) have said that, in their view, much of the 'discussion of attachment theory (in social policy) ... detracts from the perfectly sensible core argument that maltreatment is bad for the child and should stop as soon as possible' (p. 2). White and Wastell have also argued that this kind of reference to attachment theory, especially in combination with neurological research, has contributed to some unwelcome social policy developments, such that the primary focus of child protection social work in England is now on 'rescuing the child' from his or her damaging environment rather than on providing help and support to families and communities. On the other hand, there are others, such as Brown and Ward (2012) and Ward and Brown (2013), who suggest that making reference to attachment theory when discussing *child maltreatment* is often entirely appropriate, especially with regards to emotional abuse where the immediate harm to the child may be harder to perceive than when considering physical or sexual abuse.

KEY TEXTS

- Brown, R. and Ward, H. (2012) 'Decision-Making within a Child's Timeframe. An Overview of Current Research Evidence for Family Justice Professionals Concerning Child Development and the Impact of Maltreatment' (Childhood Wellbeing Research Centre). Available at https://www.gov.uk/government/uploads/system/uploads/attachment_data/file/200471/Decision-making_within_a_child_s_timeframe.pdf
- Ward, H. and Brown, R. (2013) 'Decision-Making within a Child's Timeframe: A Response', *Family Law*, 43 (September): pp. 1181–1186
- Waters, E. and McIntosh, J. (2011) 'Are We Asking the Right Questions about Attachment?', *Family Court Review*, 49 (3): pp. 474–482
- White, S. and Wastell, D. (unpublished, 2013) 'A Response to Brown, R. and Ward, H. 'Decision-Making within a Child's Timeframe'. Available at http://www.14gis.co.uk/documents/Response_to_Brown_and_Ward_17th_June.pdf

mothers

SEE ALSO fathers; gender

In the *history of attachment theory and research*, it would certainly appear to be the case that far more research has been conducted with mothers (and about 'mothering') than with other caring adults. However, it is important not to confuse this historical fact with an interpretation of attachment theory as being solely or even mainly related to mothers. To understand why *Bowlby* wrote primarily about mothers, at least in his earlier writings, one would probably not need to look much further than the prevailing social and cultural norms of the time and location in which he was writing. Bowlby was a product of his time in terms of the values he exhibited regarding *parenting*, although it is interesting to note that empirical research on child–father attachment relationships started before Bowlby published the first of his ground-breaking trilogy on attachment, separation and loss in 1969. Nevertheless, there are many examples of early writings regarding attachment theory that did not refer to *fathers* (or other potential attachment figures) and referred only to mothers. More recently, attachment research has been undertaken in most countries and cultures worldwide, involving many different actual or potential attachment figures, including fathers, grandparents, foster carers, adoptive carers, siblings, other family members (particularly relevant for children in *kinship care*) and with regards to *multiple attachments*. Attachment theory has also been applied to many different kinds of family and caring arrangements, including nuclear families, multi-generational families, reconstituted families, collectives and more, although as we mentioned in other sections, there is still much more work to do in these areas.

However, insofar as mothers in many cultures continue to fulfil the role of primary carer and insofar as there is a perspective within attachment theory that considers the baby's first attachment figure as playing a special role in the development of *internal working models*, this suggests, by dint of practical arrangement, that mothers may often be distinctive figures worthy of special consideration. Many may also take the view that mothers and fathers play different but complementary roles in terms of their influence on the child although, of course, these two viewpoints are not mutually exclusive. Evidence of the potentially special relevance of the child–mother attachment relationship can be found in some of the early research findings involving the *Strange Situation Procedure*. For example, Main and Weston (1981) found that it is entirely possible for the infant to have discordant attachment relationships with their mother and their father. Interestingly, it is estimated that around half of children have *secure attachment* relationships with their mother and father (concordant), nearly one-fifth have *insecure attachment* relationships to both (also concordant) and the remainder, over one-third, are estimated to have a secure attachment relationship with one and an insecure attachment relationship with the other (discordant).

Nevertheless, even though much of this research has been highly gendered, the infant–mother attachment relationship is currently the stronger predictor of the infant's response to the stranger (in the *Strange Situation Procedure*) than the nature of the infant–father attachment relationship. Furthermore, whilst both associations are statistically highly significant, there is a stronger relationship between the mother's state of mind with regards attachment and the infant's internal working models of attachment than with the father's (van IJzendoorn and De Wolff, 1997). But, of course, if fathers en masse were to become the main carers for children, these findings could be reversed (and if this were true, any mother/father attachment-related differences would primarily relate to socially-conditioned *gender* roles rather than to biology per se). Additionally, the majority of attachment research to date has included children of heterosexual couples. More recently, researchers have studied the children of lesbian and gay parents and these studies have suggested that there are no significant attachment-related differences for the children of homosexual primary carers. For example, Erich *et al.* (2009) found that adolescent attachment was unrelated to the sexual orientation of the child's attachment figure, whereas Golombok and Badger (2010) actually found that children from 'mother-headed' families (with a single female carer or a lesbian couple) showed lower levels of *separation protest* than children from other kinds of families (see Golombok and Badger, 2010), although why this should be the case is not yet clear.

KEY TEXTS

- Erich, S., Kanenberg, H., Case, K., Allen, T. and Bogdanos, T. (2009) 'An Empirical Analysis of Factors Affecting Adolescent Attachment in Adoptive Families with Homosexual and Straight Parents', *Children and Youth Services Review*, 31 (3): pp. 398–404
- Golombok, S. and Badger, S. (2010) 'Children Raised in Mother-headed Families from Infancy: A Follow-Up of Children of Lesbian and Single Heterosexual Mothers, at Early Adulthood', *Human Reproduction*, 25 (1): pp. 150–157
- Main, M. and Weston, D. (1981) 'The Quality of the Toddler's Relationship to Mother and to Father: Related to Conflict Behavior and the Readiness to Establish New Relationships', *Child Development*, 52 (3): pp. 932–940

multiple attachments

SEE ALSO fathers; history of attachment theory and research; kinship care; mothers

When John *Bowlby* first started writing about attachment, although he did not explicitly exclude the development of multiple attachment relationships, he did argue that children are born with an innate need to develop one primary attachment with one primary carer. As a consequence of the social values and norms of his time, Bowlby argued that this would usually, if not always, be with the child's mother. This idea, known as monotropy, places special emphasis on the child's first primary attachment relationship, suggesting that whilst the child might develop other attachment relationships, there would remain something special, something qualitatively different, about this first relationship in particular. This led in turn to the development of Bowlby's hypothesis of maternal deprivation, the proposal that the child's first attachment relationship is of such special significance that a failure to develop or maintain it would lead to serious and negative consequences for the child. The potential implications of this hypothesis are wide-ranging. For example, one (mistaken) implication could be that *mothers* should not leave their child for any extended period of time before the child is around five years of age. This in turn could be (mistakenly) interpreted as suggesting that mothers should not return to work before this time and that the child should not be placed into day care.

However, it is easy to challenge these ideas, not least from a feminist perspective, by noting that these hypotheses at the very least seem to place mothers under (more) pressure than *fathers* to remain at home. In addition, such ideas are challenged by attachment theory itself. For example, in the 1960s, it was discovered that by around 18 months of age, only a small minority of children are attached to only one person. These findings would seem to cast serious doubt on the assertion that the child's first attachment relationship is of such vital importance. In the late 1970s, Rutter (1979) further challenged these hypotheses when he noted that children often respond to separation from different attachment figures in similar ways. In other words, from the child's behaviour, it is not necessarily apparent that one of their attachment relationships is qualitatively different from (or more important than) any others. Rutter also argued that Bowlby failed to distinguish sufficiently between 'privation', which he defined as a failure to form an attachment bond at all, and 'deprivation', which he defined as temporary or permanent separation from an attachment figure. Another criticism of the idea of monotropy is that only in very limited circumstances, if any, is it reasonable to consider mothers to be the sole carers for their children, even if in many situations they might be the primary carer. In other words, holding mothers solely responsible for the child's development is not only highly likely to be damaging, at both the individual and the social level, but it is also inaccurate in empirical terms as well.

Thus, the current position within attachment theory is that children will usually form multiple attachment relationships, and that whilst there may be a hierarchy within them, that is, the child may preferentially seek out proximity with one particular primary carer if given the choice, it is unlikely that one attachment relationship is so unique for the child that any rupture or difficulty with it will automatically lead to negative consequences.

With regards to *adult attachment*, Doherty and Feeney (2004) found that for many, a romantic partner will fulfil the role of 'primary attachment figure' but, as with children, it is usually possible to identify a network of attachment figures, often including mothers, fathers, siblings, (adult) children and close friends, with the structure of this network being related to variables such as the adult's age, their relationship status and their parental status.

KEY TEXTS

- Doherty, N. and Feeney, J. (2004) 'The Composition of Attachment Networks throughout the Adult Years', *Journal of Personal Relationships*, 11 (4): pp. 469–488
- Rutter, M. (1979) 'Maternal Deprivation, 1972–78: New Findings, New Concepts, New Approaches', *Child Development*, 50 (2): pp. 283–305
- Smith, P. (1980) 'Shared Care of Younger Children: Alternative Models to Monotropism', *Merrill-Palmer Quarterly*, 26 (4): pp. 371–389

n

nature and nurture arguments

SEE ALSO evolutionary insights; gender; genetic influences

The debate regarding the relative influence of nature and nurture on human development is an age-old one. The idea that humans might be primarily, or even exclusively, a product of their environments (nurture) can be found in the writings of the Greek philosopher, Aristotle. The concept of a baby as a 'tabula rasa', a blank slate, was further developed in the eleventh, twelfth and thirteenth centuries and is perhaps best captured in the Jesuit motto 'Give me a child until he is seven and I will give you the man' (meaning that any child could be 'moulded' by the age of seven, depending on their environment). More recently, in the twentieth century, Sigmund Freud argued that many adult personality traits result primarily from the child's early family history. However, following the publication of 'On the Origin of Species' by Charles Darwin in 1859, the possibility that human development was, at least in part, based upon hereditary inheritance was given an increasingly scientific footing. The modern evolutionary synthesis of the twentieth century, in which a growing knowledge of genetics was combined with the study of animal populations, made it all the more difficult to justify a view of humans as 'blank slates' at birth. Thus, it became increasingly clear that our genes play at least some part in all areas of human development. Indeed, some suggested that human development was primarily under the control of our genes and that nurture – the influence of environmental factor – has only a minimal influence (see Pinker, 2003). Despite the often-politicized nature of this debate, there has been an increasing tendency to frame this issue in terms of an interaction between nature and nurture (rather than it being a case of 'either-or'). For example, Ridley (2004) has described human development as 'nature via nurture'.

However, in many popular discussions of nature or nurture (or nature via nurture), several important aspects of heritability are often overlooked. Firstly, heritability describes how far our genes are responsible for trait variations amongst a given population. And secondly, there is an important distinction between explaining the variation among traits and explaining the causation of traits. For example, in order to start a fire, one needs a combined source of heat, fuel and oxygen and although there are many situations in which fuel and oxygen are combined without combusting, if from this we concluded that it is only the source of heat that explains the presence or absence of fire, this would be a mistake. In other words, the source of heat may explain (some of) the variation in combustion but it cannot explain the presence or absence of fire. Applied to human development, it is therefore relatively easy to confuse variation among traits as being primarily influenced by nature or nurture with an understanding that the trait itself is caused primarily by our genes or our environment.

KEY TEXTS

- Belsky, J. and Pluess, M. (2009) 'Beyond Diathesis Stress: Differential Susceptibility to Environmental Influences', *Psychological Bulletin*, 135 (6): pp. 885–908
- Pinker, S. (2003) *The Blank Slate: The Modern Denial of Human Nature* (London: Penguin)
- Ridley, M. (2004) *Nature via Nurture: Genes, Experiences and What Makes Us Human* (New York: HarperCollins)

neglected children

SEE ALSO **child maltreatment; disorganized attachment**

When discussing *child maltreatment*, a distinction is often drawn between abuse and neglect, with abuse referring to the 'active' harm of a child and neglect referring to more 'passive' harm, to the absence of 'good enough' care in one or more areas. However, the idea of neglect as somehow 'passive' is not to suggest it is less problematic for children. Indeed, there is a large body of evidence to confirm that neglectful care, especially long-standing neglectful care, is associated with a variety of very negative outcomes and difficulties for children. In particular, neglectful care is associated with higher rates of *insecure attachment* relationships and *disorganized attachment* behaviour, even when compared with children from 'high-risk' but non-maltreating backgrounds (Cyr *et al.*, 2010).

When considering the precursors of neglectful behaviour in carers, there appears to be a correlation between the carer's history of insecure attachment relationships in childhood and adulthood, especially when found in combination with childhood experiences of *unresolved loss and trauma*. Crittenden, who has studied child neglect extensively, has consistently found that the attachment figures of neglected children are also less likely to demonstrate *attunement and sensitivity* in their caregiving behaviour.

More recently, attachment researchers have attempted to understand in detail the relationship between particular kinds of neglect and developmental outcomes for children. For example, Stronach and colleagues (2011) considered whether different kinds of neglect (or abuse) – as measured by the type, chronicity, severity and frequency – might impact differently on the child's development of a *secure attachment* or insecure attachment relationship to an attachment figure and on the prevalence of disorganized attachment behaviour. They found that whilst children who were not neglected (or abused) had higher rates of secure attachment, lower rates of disorganized attachment behaviour and more positive *internal working models*, the type of maltreatment (whether abuse or neglect), the chronicity, the severity and the frequency appeared to make little or no difference (in these specific areas). In other words, they could detect no significant differences in the security or insecurity, or the organization or disorganization of the child's attachment relationships, regardless of whether the child was neglected as opposed to abused, and regardless of the chronicity, severity or frequency of the maltreatment. This may suggest that there is something fundamental about the impact of neglect (and abuse) on the child's attachment relationship, with the nature of the neglect perhaps leading to different outcomes in ways unrelated to attachment.

KEY TEXTS
- Cyr, C., Euser, E., Bakermans-Kranenburg, M. and van IJzendoorn, M. (2010) 'Attachment Security and Disorganization in Maltreating and High-Risk Families: A Series of Meta-analyses', *Development and Psychopathology*, 22 (1): pp. 87–108

- Stoltenborgh, M., Bakermans-Kranenburg, M. and van IJzendoorn, M. (2013) 'The Neglect of Child Neglect: A Meta-analytic Review of the Prevalence of Neglect', *Social Psychiatry and Psychiatric Epidemiology*, 48 (3): pp. 345–355
- Stronach, E., Toth, S., Rogosch, F., Oshri, A., Manly, J. and Cicchetti, D. (2011) 'Child Maltreatment, Attachment Security and Internal Representations of Mother and Mother–Child Relationships', *Child Maltreatment*, 16 (2): pp. 137–145

O

object relations theory

SEE ALSO history of attachment theory and research; mothers

Object relations theory is a term used to describe a relatively diverse group of psychological theories in which people are viewed as having an internal, often unconscious, construction of relationships. Object relations theory postulates that our external experience of relationships becomes internalized in our (unconscious) mind, within which mental representations of others ('objects') and of the self (the 'subject') interact and become intertwined. In this fashion we all carry unconscious impressions of our relationships and of ourselves in relation to others and these mental constructs influence our relationships in the external world (see *memory*). Another key idea within object relations theory is that people have a primary need for close relationships with other people in order to realize an understanding of 'the self'. Both of these ideas have been influential in the *history of attachment theory and research* and particularly in the development of the concept of *internal working models*. In many ways, contemporary attachment theory could be understood as a development of object relations theory (or perhaps a specialized subset of it).

Melanie Klein (1882–1960), influenced by the work of Sigmund Freud, is commonly identified with the development of object relations theory (much as *Bowlby* is with regards to attachment theory). Klein described many of the key themes within the theory, such as phantasy (the unconscious version of fantasy), projective identification and the paranoid–schizoid and depressive relational positions. Klein argued that early interactions between babies and their *mothers* are so intense and so full of meaning that the ways and processes by which these interactions are resolved, especially when they involve conflict, will be reflected in the development of the adult personality. Klein, in a departure from Freud, claimed that people primarily sought satisfaction through their relationships with others, rather than by the gratification of biological and psychological urges (or drives).

Winnicott (1956) described the intense bond between a mother and her baby as a 'primary (maternal) preoccupation' and as a 'normal illness', in the sense that were this bond not so common, it might be seen as an abnormality. Winnicott argued that this bond begins when the baby is in utero and helps the baby's transition into the external world. Winnicott also believed that the mother's role was to ensure the baby experienced this 'primary preoccupation' (with her) sufficiently enough to feel 'held' and safe but not so intensely as to prevent the development of a sense of distinctiveness. Winnicott identified the use of transitional objects by infants as a way of helping them become more independent, objects such as a blanket or a soft toy. Winnicott saw how children will often carry such objects around with them, seemingly in order to help them cope with being away from their mother.

Notably, Winnicott (1992) also appears to have coined the phrase 'good enough' *parenting*, an idiom often used by child and family social workers; when Winnicott used it, he meant specifically the provision of sufficient contact by the primary carer so as to enable the child to feel 'held' but not so tightly as to prevent them from exploring the wider world as part of a process of individuation.

KEY TEXTS

- Kosciejew, R. (2013) *Object Relations Theory* (Bloomington, IN: AuthorHouse)
- Winnicott, D. (1956) 'Primary Maternal Preoccupation' in *Through Paediatrics to Psychoanalysis* (London: Hogarth)
- Winnicott, D. (1992) *The Child, The Family and the Outside World*. 2nd edn (New York: Perseus Publishing)

p

parenting

SEE ALSO fathers; fostering and adoption; kinship care; mothers

Parenting may be commonly defined as simply being the mother or father of a child or children and in many ways, parenting can appear to be supremely uncomplicated, having clearly been a feature of human behaviour and society since humans first evolved. Indeed in a much broader sense, parenting behaviour has surely been in existence since the first organisms evolved reproductive strategies reliant on having relatively few offspring and providing a relatively high investment in their survival. However, as with many aspects of human behaviour, what may at first appear to be an uncomplicated endeavour very quickly becomes more nuanced and complex the more one considers it. For example, in many cultures, parenting will involve the promotion and support of a child in his or her physical, emotional, social and intellectual development from birth, well into adolescence and beyond. There are also many different ways to parent, not only when comparisons are made across cultures, but within the same culture, without any one set of parenting behaviours being unequivocally optimal when compared with any other set of parenting behaviours (Laraeu, 2002).

However, despite the great variety of ways one may behave as a parent, Diana Baumrind, a development psychologist, has conceptualized this great variety as representing just one of four parenting styles – authoritative, authoritarian, permissive and uninvolved (see Figure 3).

Authoritative parenting is said to involve 'responsive demands' by the parent on the child, relying on positive reinforcement of desirable behaviour and little or no punishment of undesirable behaviour. Authoritative parents tend to have well-developed abilities of *mentalization and reflective function* and they are supportive of their child's development of autonomy, *exploration and security.*

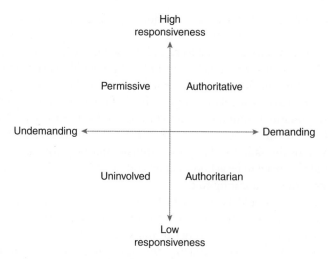

FIGURE 3   *Four styles of parenting and their relationship with the scales of demanding–undemanding and responsive–unresponsive*

Authoritarian parenting, on the other hand, is more rigid, with high demands placed on the child, accompanied by a lower level of responsiveness to their needs. Punishment is often a common feature of this style and may lead to the child feeling less secure and more vulnerable to stress.

Permissive parenting places a high value on the child's autonomy and freedom and there is little or no punishment of the child. Permissive parents tend to be undemanding of the child and may have few explicit rules about what the child should do or should not do.

Finally, uninvolved parenting describes parents who may be emotionally or physically absent from the child for significant periods of time. This parenting style may seem similar to the situation experienced by *neglected children*, at least to some degree.

Karavasillis and her colleagues (2003) compared these four parenting styles with attachment patterns and found that authoritative parenting was most positively associated with *secure attachment* whilst uninvolved parenting was most positively associated with *avoidant attachment* relationships. However, these researchers also found a unique pattern of association between particular elements of parenting and attachment relationships, highlighting the need to be clear about the distinction between parenting as an overall set of behaviours and practices, and caregiving behaviour, that is, specific responses to attachment bids by the child, as conceptualized within attachment theory. For example, a child may have an *insecure attachment* relationship with his father and yet receive a lot of pleasure through play and stimulation from him. Whilst the insecure nature of the attachment may need to be addressed (or it may not), the father's ability to stimulate and play with the child would also need to be acknowledged and regarded as a key strength of the father's parenting role.

Finally, it should be noted that parenting is often a contested concept, especially from a sociological perspective. Expectations as to what *mothers, fathers* or other primary carers of children 'should' or 'should not' do will inevitably flex and change over time and in addition, parenting may also be conceived of differently, depending on the family's ethnicity, social class and wealth.

KEY TEXTS

- Baumrind, D. (1967) 'Child Care Practices Anteceding Three Patterns of Preschool Behavior', *Genetic Psychology Monographs*, 75 (1): pp. 43–88
- Karavasillis, L., Doyle, A. and Markiewicz, D. (2003) 'Associations between Parenting Style and Attachment to Mother in Middle Childhood and Adolescence', *International Journal of Behavioral Development*, 27 (2): pp. 153–164
- Lareau, A. (2002) 'Invisible Inequality: Social Class and Childrearing in Black Families and White Families', *American Sociological Review*, 67 (5): pp. 747–776

proximity-seeking and safe-haven behaviours

SEE ALSO **goal-oriented behaviour; secure base; separation protest**

Separation protest, safe-haven behaviour, *secure base* behaviour and proximity-seeking behaviour are all key features of a child–adult attachment relationship, with *Bowlby* describing the balance for the child between *exploration and security* as being akin to a homeostatic control system. In other words, children will tend to use a mixture of behaviours to manage their own internal sense of anxiety or fear. Thus, as the child's sense of anxiety increases, so the child will tend to display increasing levels of separation protest and a concomitant 'activation' of proximity-seeking behaviours, with the aim of achieving a level of proximity with a safe haven, as represented by their attachment figure. As the child's sense of anxiety reduces, so their level of separation protest and proximity-seeking behaviours will also tend to reduce, in turn allowing for an increase in playful or exploratory behaviour.

The child's expectation and understanding of their attachment figure as a 'safe haven' to return to during times of heightened anxiety is one of the most significant aspects that distinguishes an attachment relationship from any other kind of close relationship, and it also marks out those animals with attachment needs from those without. Most animals prefer to return to a safe place when feeling threatened but animals with attachment needs tend to prefer to return to an older member of their species (an attachment figure). Of course, not all children perceive their attachment figures to be a safe haven and this may especially apply in the case of *neglected children* and *child maltreatment*. In these situations, the child may experience 'fear without solution' (both wanting and fearing proximity with the attachment figure) and display *disorganized attachment* behaviour as a result.

KEY TEXTS

- Ainsworth, M. and Bell, S. (1970) 'Attachment, Exploration, and Separation: Illustrated by the Behavior of One-Year-Olds in a Strange Situation', *Child Development*, 41 (4): pp. 49–67
- Collins, N., Feeney, B. and Brooke, C. (2000) 'A Safe Haven: An Attachment Theory Perspective on Support Seeking and Caregiving in Intimate Relationships', *Journal of Personality and Social Psychology*, 78 (6): pp. 1053–1073
- Feeney, B. and Collins, N. (2004) 'Interpersonal Safe Haven and Secure Base Caregiving Processes in Adulthood' in W. Rholes and J. Simpson (eds), *Adult Attachment: Theory, Research and Clinical Implications* (New York: Guilford Press): pp. 300–338

psychopathology and mental ill health

SEE ALSO (reactive) attachment disorder; child maltreatment; disorganized attachment; neglected children; risk and resilience factors; unresolved loss and trauma

Attachment theory is both a theory of normal development and a theory of psychopathological development. In other words, it is not only a theory about how all humans tend to develop but also a theory about how (and why) development may 'go wrong' (Sroufe *et al.*, 1999). Although difficult early relational experiences do not have a linear causal relationship with the subsequent development of psychopathological symptomology and mental ill health, they may serve to initiate or 'promote' certain developmental pathways probabilistically associated with the appearance of psychopathological symptomology and mental ill health. Thus, whilst *insecure attachment* and even *disorganized attachment* behaviour are not considered to be pathological, they may often be correlated with pathological development. This understanding has led to an increasing interest, both from a research perspective but also clinically, in how attachment processes, along with other aspects of development, might help to elucidate the aetiologies of specific psychopathological symptoms including hallucinations and delusions (Read and Bentall, 2012). On the other hand, *secure attachment* may offer a degree of resilience against potential future difficulties. In particular, some *interventions* aimed at boosting attachment security have been found to have beneficial effects for mental health and in other areas as well. Thus, attachment may play a dual role in the understanding of both risk and resilience factors.

However, mental ill health and psychopathology are far from homogenous phenomena, whether in an objective or subjective sense. Thus, it is not surprising that for specific conditions or disorders, including attachment disorder, there may be found more or less evidence of a positive association with attachment, and different studies will report different findings in relation to the same issue. For example, with regards to depression, some studies have found a link between depressive symptoms and insecure forms of *adult attachment* but other studies have not, especially when using the *Adult Attachment Interview* as the research measure. However, when using *self-report measures of attachment*, more consistent data have emerged of depressive symptoms being positively associated with preoccupied and fearful attachment and negatively associated with secure attachment. This may initially suggest that the Adult Attachment Interview and self-report measures of attachment are 'accessing' different aspects of attachment. In any event, whether this association is causal – and if so, in which direction – is difficult to establish (even if one accepts that studies using self-report measures of attachment have sufficient validity). Does depressive symptomology contribute to higher levels of attachment insecurity or do higher levels of attachment insecurity contribute to more depressive symptomology? Or do attachment insecurity and depressive symptomology tend to coincide because of other co-existing variables? At present, there appears to be insufficient data to provide conclusive answers to these and other questions.

Similarly, anxiety disorders are heterogeneous in nature and although *Bowlby* proposed that such disorders are best understood as resulting from chronic anxiety about the availability of attachment figures, there is very little data to support or oppose such a hypothesis, with much of the research that has been undertaken failing to distinguish between different types of anxiety disorder. Having said this, the general trend has been to identify a relatively strong association between the presence of an anxiety disorder (of unspecified type) and insecure attachment and in particular with the 'unresolved' category of adult attachment. Another example is the relationship between preoccupied adult attachment and Borderline Personality Disorder (BPD). According to Scott and colleagues (2013), although preoccupied adult attachment and difficulties with emotional dysregulation are associated with various personality disorders, they may be specifically related to an understanding of the core difficulties experienced by people with BPD, including overwhelming feelings of distress, anxiety and worthlessness, difficulties in the self-management of emotions and in maintaining close relationships.

Another aspect of the complex relationship between attachment and mental ill health can be seen in the interplay between these two phenomena for the children of adults with mental health problems. One question is whether and how the child's understanding of the parent's mental health problems may interact with their understanding of the parent as an attachment figure (Walsh, 2009).

Whilst it is clear that most parents with mental ill health care for their children effectively and safely, a small number of such children may be harmed (though not necessarily physically) and the quality and nature of the attachment relationship between the child and the parent has been highlighted as one possible moderating process in the relationship between risk and resilience factors.

KEY TEXTS

- Mikulincer, M. and Shaver, P. (2012) 'An Attachment Perspective on Psychopathology', *World Psychiatry*, 11 (1): pp. 11–15
- Read, J. and Bentall, J. (2012) 'Negative Childhood Experiences and Mental Health: Theoretical, Clinical and Primary Prevention Implications', *The British Journal of Psychiatry*, 200 (2): pp. 89–91
- Sroufe, L. A., Carlson, E., Levy, A. and Egeland, B. (1999) 'Implications of Attachment Theory for Developmental Psychopathology', *Development and Psychopathology*, 11 (1): pp. 1–13

r

research methods in attachment

SEE ALSO Crittenden's Dynamic-Maturational Model; history of
attachment theory and research; self-report measures of attachment

Research into the many different facets of attachment has led to
the development of a variety of research methods, many of which
are discussed elsewhere in this book, such as the *Adult Attachment
Interview, Child Attachment Interview, self-report measures of attachment, Story Stem Completion* and the *Strange Situation Procedure.*

Attachment-related research methods for young children tend
to be based on observations of their behaviour, as is the case for
the Strange Situation Procedure. However, the Strange Situation
Procedure is usually only suitable for children aged between
around 9 and 18 months of age and so other methods of observation for older children have also been developed. These include
the preschool strange situation for children aged between two and
four-and-a-half years of age, the attachment Q-set for children aged
between one and five years of age and the Preschool Assessment of
Attachment for children aged between 18 months and 5 years of age.
Together, these methods involve observations of the child, either
in different environments or following longer periods of separation than are typically used for the Strange Situation Procedure.
The rationale behind the use of longer periods of separation or
observations of children over a longer period of time is that as children grow older, they develop more sophisticated *internal working
models* and they also become more used to separations. They also
develop a greater ability to 'hold in mind' their attachment figure/s
as they progress beyond the Piagetian stage of 'object permanence', that is, they know that when their attachment figure is no
longer with them in the room, nevertheless they still exist. Thus, a
three-year-old child is unlikely to feel as anxious as quickly when
separated from their mother, father or other carer as will a typical
nine-month-old child.

Another difference between methods for older children and the Strange Situation Procedure is that for older children, the methods tend to involve an analysis not only of the child's behavioural responses to separation and reunion episodes but also an analysis of the child's use of language, especially when this relates to the child's attempts to obtain or maintain proximity to the attachment figure. Similarly, in the attachment Q-set, the child's social cognition is analysed alongside any behaviour evidencing their use of the attachment figure as a *secure base*.

For attachment-related research involving middle aged children (five to eight years of age), research methods tend to involve some form of projection, such as Story Stem Completion or picture responses techniques, which are designed to access the child's internal working models of attachment by asking them to respond to a series of attachment-related scenarios.

For attachment-related research involving older children (9–12 years of age), adolescents or adults, researchers may use semi-structured interviews designed to probe the respondent's internal working models of attachment more directly. This would include methods such as the Adult Attachment Interview and the Child Attachment Interview. These interviews tend to involve direct questions such as 'How would you describe your relationship with your mother/father?' although it is not simply the respondent's answers which are analysed but the manner in which they respond. For older age groups, self-report measures of attachment may also be used.

Taking an overview of the *history of attachment theory and research*, the Strange Situation Procedure is the most well established of all the attachment-related research methods, often referred to as the 'gold standard' of attachment research. With regards to adults, the Adult Attachment Interview is the most well established method. For many of the other methods, it is reasonable to say that further evidence is needed in order to establish the same degree of validity and reliability.

In addition to the methods outlined above, *Crittenden's Dynamic-Maturational Model* (DMM) offers an alternative basis for attachment research. Methods developed within this tradition include the Infant Strange Situation, the Preschool Assessment of Attachment, the School-Age Assessment of Attachment and an alternative approach to the completion and analysis of the Adult

Attachment Interview. The Infant Strange Situation is largely the same within the DMM as within the Ainsworth–Main tradition but in the analysis, additional categories of attachment behaviour are applied (subcategories of the organized categories of avoidant, secure and ambivalent-resistant or, in the DMM, Type A, B and C respectively). The Preschool Assessment of Attachment is a method of coding the Strange Situation Procedure for older children, aged between two and five years. The same method is used as for younger children but the analysis is again extended to include a further range of DMM subcategories. The School-Age Assessment of Attachment is a projective technique used for children aged between 6 and 12 years of age. It involves the child looking at a series of pictures depicting 'threats' (e.g. a boy being bullied). The child is asked to tell a story about the child on the card and asked if something similar has ever happened to them. The analysis is based on a combination of behavioural observations and discourse analysis. The DMM tradition also employs a modified Adult Attachment Interview, including a number of additional questions, particularly focused on the possible experiences of very troubled adults and the analysis includes the full range of DMM categories and subcategories.

The CARE-index has also developed from the DMM tradition and can be used for infants from birth to 15 months of age or for toddlers aged between 16 and 72 months of age (although this method measures the interaction between the child and an attachment figure rather than the attachment relationship of the child per se). Using the CARE-index involves taking short videos of the attachment figure playing with the child. The behaviour of both the child and the adult is analysed from a relational perspective. For example, if the child squirmed, shrieked and threw their toys, they might be coded as 'difficult' from the adult's perspective.

Compared with the Ainsworth–Main research tradition, Farnfield *et al.* (2010) note that DMM methods may be more helpful or applicable to children in 'high-risk' situations (e.g. *child maltreatment*) although they also found that for all of the DMM methods (other than the CARE-index), validation studies are needed both between the DMM methods and in comparison with other attachment-related research methods.

KEY TEXTS

- Bartholomew, K. and Moretti, M. (2002) 'The Dynamics of Measuring Attachment', *Attachment and Human Development*, 4 (2): pp. 162–165
- Farnfield, S., Hautamaki, A., Norbech, P. and Sahhar, N. (2010) 'Dynamic-Maturational Model Assessments of Attachment and Adaptation', *Clinical Child Psychology and Psychiatry*, 15 (3): pp. 313–328
- Griffin, D. and Bartholomew, K. (1994a) 'The Metaphysics of Measurement: The Case of Adult Attachment' in K. Bartholomew and D. Perlman (eds), *Attachment Processes in Adulthood* (London: Jessica Kingsley Publishers): pp. 17–52

risk and resilience factors

SEE ALSO **child maltreatment; neglected children; psychopathology and mental ill health**

Resilience is commonly understood as the ability to recover quickly from or to cope with difficulties. Psychological resilience is thus the ability to recover from or to cope with psychological-related difficulties such as stress and anxiety. The presence of a *secure attachment* relationship has been identified as one of the more significant contributory factors regarding an individual's resilience and, in Simon Baron-Cohen's evocative phrase, it appears that early experiences of a secure attachment relationship can leave you with an internal 'pot of gold' upon which to rely in later life.

Contemporary research regarding resilience and risk emerged at least to some extent from the observation that whilst some individuals exposed to difficulty and adversity achieve what might be termed normal (or adaptive) developmental outcomes, others do not. Individuals from the former group are thus said to have demonstrated a certain level of resilience. In some contexts, resilience means that the individual has returned to their 'normal state', to the state they were in prior to the difficult experience. In other contexts, resilience means that the individual has not suffered any significant negative effects as a result of the difficult experience but may nevertheless be in a changed state. In still other contexts, resilience may mean that the individual demonstrates improved functioning following a difficult experience. In any event, resilience is perhaps best conceptualized as a process rather than as a fixed characteristic, such as *temperament,* meaning that the correct nomenclature is 'resilience' rather than 'resiliency'. Protective factors are usually conceptualized as being conditions or attributes that offset, mitigate or eliminate risk factors, or those that increase the health and well-being of individuals and families. For example, a protective factor for a child living in deprived circumstances may be their experience of a high-quality education. Furthermore, there is a difference between distal and proximate risk and protective factors, between factors that are more broadly felt, such as poverty, and factors that are more specifically felt, such as caregiving behaviour or family structure.

In the context of attachment theory, resilience has often been shown to correlate positively with secure attachment and negatively with *insecure attachment.* The presence of *attunement and sensitivity* on the part of an attachment figure has also been suggested as a protective factor for children and again, often correlates positively with better outcomes in later life, such as educational achievements and an increased ability to cope with stress. However, the relationship between resilience, attachment security and protective factors is a complicated one. For example, does a secure attachment relationship lead to increased resilience or does the absence of difficult experiences make it more likely that the child will develop a secure attachment relationship (see Owens and Shaw, 2003; Riggs and Riggs, 2011)?

KEY TEXTS

- Jenson, J. and Fraser, M. (2011) *Social Policy for Children and Families: A Risk and Resilience Perspective.* 2nd edn (London: Sage Publications)
- Marriner, P., Caciolli, J. and Moore, K. (2014) 'The Relationship of Attachment to Resilience and Their Impact on Perceived Stress' in K. Kaniasty, K. Moore, S. Howard and P. Buchwald (eds), *Stress and Anxiety* (Berlin: Logos Verlag): pp. 73–82
- Owens, E. and Shaw, D. (2003) 'Poverty and Early Childhood Adjustment' in S. Luthar (ed.), *Resilience and Vulnerability: Adaptation in the Context of Childhood Adversities* (Cambridge: Cambridge University Press): pp. 267–292

romantic attachments

SEE ALSO adult attachment; attachment relationships in adulthood; self-report measures of attachment

Some of the earliest and most significant research into *adult attachment* concerned attachment relationships between romantic partners. In 1987, Hazan and Shaver reported that they had identified *secure attachment, ambivalent-resistant attachment* and *avoidant attachment* relationships between romantic partners. In order to explore these relationships, Hazan and Shaver used *self-report measures of attachment* and found that 55 per cent of the adults in their research had a secure state of mind with regards to attachment, 25 per cent an avoidant state of mind and 20 per cent an ambivalent-resistant state of mind. Further research into romantic attachments indicated that a secure state of mind was often characterized by a positive image of the self and of others; the avoidant state of mind by a negative image of the self and of others, and the ambivalent-resistant state of mind by a negative image of the self and a positive image of others (fearful states of mind imply that both images are negative). Given these conceptualizations, it is unsurprising to find that adults with avoidant states of mind tend to feel more pessimistic about long-term relationships and to have higher rates of separation and divorce, whereas adults with ambivalent-resistant states of mind tend to express a strong desire for romantic intimacy but may find it harder to develop a trusting, long-term relationship. Perhaps as a result, they also tend to have higher rates of separation and divorce. Adults with secure states of mind tend to seek out longer-term relationships and to report higher levels of relational satisfaction. Similar data in this regard has been found for homosexual romantic relationships as for heterosexual romantic relationships.

Pietromonaco, DeBuse and Powers (2013) argue that romantic attachment insecurity in general predicts differential stress responses and even more so when the reason for the increased stress relates to a perceived threat to the relationship. In other words, just as children respond to stress in their environment by 'turning to' their attachment figure in particular ways, based on their *internal working models*, so adults in a romantic relationship may 'activate' their attachment system in response to (perceived) threats to the relationship itself (such as one partner threatening to leave).

KEY TEXTS

- Hazen, C. and Shaver, P. (1987) 'Romantic Love Conceptualized as an Attachment Process', *Journal of Personality and Social Psychology*, 52 (3): pp. 511–524
- Mikulincer, M. and Goodman, G. (eds) (2006) *Dynamics of Romantic Love: Attachment, Caregiving and Sex* (New York: Guilford Press)
- Pietromonaco, P., DeBuse, C. and Powers, S. (2013) 'Does Attachment Get under the Skin? Adult Romantic Attachment and Cortisol Responses to Stress', *Current Directions in Psychological Science*, 22 (1): pp. 63–68

S

secure attachment

SEE ALSO ambivalent-resistant attachment; avoidant attachment;
disorganized attachment; insecure attachment

Would you tend to agree or disagree with the following statements?

- I find it relatively easy to get close to others.
- I am comfortable depending on them and having them depend
  on me.
- I don't worry about being abandoned or about someone getting
  too close to me.

If you agreed with these statements (see *self-report measures of attachment*), you may have a secure state of mind with regards to attachment. According to several large-scale and cross-cultural studies of typical populations, around 60–65 per cent of adults have a secure state of mind (Bakermans-Kranenburg and van IJzendoorn, 2009) and around 60–65 per cent of children have secure attachment relationships (van IJzendoorn and Kroonenberg, 1988). There are some *cultural differences* in these distributions between different populations but for the most part, these are not particularly significant.

As with the infant categories of *ambivalent-resistant attachment* and *avoidant attachment*, the category of secure attachment was first discovered using the *Strange Situation Procedure*. When Mary Ainsworth first devised the Strange Situation Procedure, along with a number of colleagues, she predicted that infants would behave differently towards their carers on separation and following reunion, and that these infants would also behave differently in terms of how they explored the room and played with the toys. What she did not predict was that it would be possible to categorize the majority of infants into just three types of attachment (secure-attachment, ambivalent-resistant attachment and avoidant attachment). In these original experiments, a number of children proved impossible to classify and it was from further studies of this group of children that the concept of *disorganized attachment* behaviour would arise).

Were you to observe an infant in the Strange Situation Procedure and they have a secure attachment relationship with their attachment figure, you would tend to see the child displaying *proximity-seeking and safe-haven* behaviour towards the attachment figure. The child would also use them as a *secure base* from which to explore and the ease with which these children are able to do so is thought to be indicative of the confidence they have in the attachment figure's ability and availability to provide care and protection. Thus, in the Strange Situation Procedure, a child with a secure attachment relationship will tend to explore and play more and to exhibit distress for shorter periods of time than other, less securely attached children (although they will still tend to be distressed upon separation from the attachment figure).

Bowlby (and others) theorized that all children develop *internal working models* of attachment and in the case of children with secure attachment relationships, this model essentially says 'it is okay for you to feel distressed and upset because your attachment figure will, in most cases, offer you the comfort you need'. When studying the behaviour of the attachment figures of infants with secure attachment relationships, it is relatively clear that they tend to offer reliable comfort to the child, that they offer *attunement and sensitivity.* Studies outside of the Strange Situation Procedure have confirmed the presence of similar caregiving behaviours in the home environment as well.

In adults, the phraseology of secure attachment is retained (although it is sometimes referred to as the 'balanced' pattern of attachment), unlike for avoidant attachment and ambivalent-resistant attachment (where the phrases 'dismissing' or 'fearful-avoidant' and 'preoccupied' tend to be used instead). Adults with a secure state of mind with regards to attachment will tend to identify the importance of close relationships and will be comfortable with the idea of their own dependency on others and of others' dependency on them. However, there is a distinction made between adults who are 'continuous secure' and adults who are 'earned secure'. As Pearson *et al.* (1994) have described, adults who describe difficult early relationships with their attachment figures but who evidently have a secure state of mind with regards to attachment now may be considered to have 'earned' (we prefer 'acquired') their security. In contrast, adults who describe both current and historical secure attachment relationships may be considered to have had 'continuous' security.

KEY TEXTS

- Pearson, J., Cohn, D., Cowan, P. and Cowan, C. (1994) 'Earned- and Continuous-Security in Adult Attachment: Relation to Depressive Symptomology and Parenting Style', *Development and Psychopathology*, 6 (2): pp. 359–373
- Silver, M. (2013) *Attachment in Common Sense and Doodles: A Practical Guide* (London: Jessica Kingsley Publishers)
- Waters, E., Merrick, S., Treboux, D., Crowell, J. and Albersheim, L. (2000) 'Attachment Security in Infancy and Early Childhood: A Twenty Year Longitudinal Study', *Child Development*, 71 (3): pp. 684–689

secure base

SEE ALSO **attunement and sensitivity; goal-oriented behaviour; proximity-seeking and safe-haven behaviours**

The concept of the secure base was one of the earliest insights in the *history of attachment theory and research* and it remains central to contemporary attachment theory as well (see Bowlby, 2005). Indeed, it is arguably between and within the interplay of *proximity-seeking and safe-haven behaviours* and secure base behaviour that the quality and nature of the individual's attachment relationships and experiences is located.

When studying infants and their attachment figures in the *Strange Situation Procedure*, Mary Ainsworth (and others) observed how infants often demonstrated particular types of behaviour towards their attachment figure following periods of separation. The differences between these kinds of behaviour helped these early attachment researchers to describe the infant attachment patterns of *ambivalent-resistant attachment, avoidant attachment* and *secure attachment*. However, in addition to behavioural differences between infants following periods of separation, Ainsworth and her colleagues also noticed how different children behaved differently in the presence of their attachment figure. Some children, those who were categorized as having secure attachment relationships, tended to demonstrate much greater confidence in their playful and exploratory behaviour, including at times following periods of separation and subsequent reunion. Other children, those who were categorized as having *insecure attachment* relationships, tended to demonstrate less confidence and greater levels of reluctance to return to play and exploration, especially following the first period of separation. As Ainsworth and others would describe, it appeared as if the children with insecure attachment relationships were demonstrating a restricted ability to return to play and exploration because of an increased anxiety about their attachment figure. These children seemed to spend more time worrying about the availability of their attachment figure than they did about playing and exploring. Children with secure attachment relationships, on the other hand, appeared to have more confidence in the availability of their attachment figures, even after two or three periods of brief separation, and thus were more able to play and explore, trusting that if they did become anxious again in future, their attachment figure would be available to soothe and comfort them. Thus, attachment is not simply 'about' the ability of the child's attachment figure to provide suitably sensitive care at times of heightened anxiety but it also affects the child's ability to explore the wider environment (see Waters *et al.*, 2002). For example, a three-year-old child who, when out in the local park, spends her whole time playing on the swings and other equipment with barely a look at her father, may well be demonstrating far greater degrees of *exploration and security* than the three-year-old who cannot bear to leave her father's side.

Given the central importance of the concept of the secure base within attachment theory as applied to children, it is not surprising that it has been applied to *adult attachment* as well. For example, Davila and Kashy (2009) studied the secure base within the context of heterosexual romantic relationships. In these kinds of adult-to-adult relationships, both individuals may be in the position of being an attachment figure and a caregiver simultaneously, suggesting that both will need to be 'capable' of seeking and providing support, in contrast with infant-to-adult attachment relationships, where the infant would not be expected to provide support for the adult. Davila and Kashy found that secure *romantic attachments*, those characterized by higher levels of comfort with intimacy and lower levels of anxiety regarding abandonment, were associated with the most adaptive experiences of support for both partners. Insecure romantic attachments, on the other hand, those characterized by lower levels of comfort with intimacy and higher levels of anxiety regarding abandonment, were associated with less adaptive experiences of support.

KEY TEXTS
- Bowlby, J. (2005) *A Secure Base.* Re-issue edn (London: Routledge)
- Clulow, C. (ed.) (2001) *Adult Attachment and Couple Psychotherapy: The 'Secure Base' in Practice and Research* (London: Routledge)
- Waters, E. and Cummings, M. (2000) 'A Secure Base from which to Explore Close Relationships', *Child Development*, 71 (1): pp. 164–172

self-report measures of attachment

SEE ALSO history of attachment theory and research; measures of attachment; research methods in attachment

In 'Romantic Love Conceptualized as an Attachment Process', Hazan and Shaver (1987) described the use of a new self-report measure of attachment in order to investigate the nature of *romantic attachments*. Hazan and Shaver's self-report measure was the first such tool to be developed and was based upon the infant attachment patterns of *secure attachment, avoidant attachment* and *ambivalent-resistant attachment*. Hazan and Shaver described these three patterns in relation to adult romantic attachments as follows:

Secure – I find it relatively easy to get close to others and am comfortable depending on them and having them depend on me. I don't worry about being abandoned or about someone getting too close to me.

Avoidant – I am somewhat uncomfortable being close to others. I find it difficult to trust them completely, difficult to allow myself to depend on them. I am nervous when anyone gets too close, and often others want to be more intimate with me than I feel comfortable with.

Ambivalent-resistant – I find that others are reluctant to get as close as I would like. I often worry that my partner doesn't really love me or won't want to stay with me. I want to get very close to my partner, and this sometimes scares people away.

As a respondent, the process of using this measure simply involves choosing which description best captures how you feel about relationships. Since the development of this simple self-report measure, a number of other measures have been developed, most of which are more complicated. For example, some self-report measures breakdown the above descriptions into numerous 'agree–disagree' items, meaning that they can be scored as continuous scales rather than discreet descriptions (Brennan, Clark and Shaver, 1998; Fraley *et al.*, 2006). This process led to the creation of a two-dimensional model of *adult attachment* based on avoidance and anxiety. Secure attachment represents low avoidance and anxiety; preoccupied attachment (similar to, but not the same as, infant ambivalent-resistant attachment) represents low avoidance and high anxiety; dismissing-avoidant (similar to, but not the same as, infant avoidant attachment) represents high avoidance and low anxiety; and a further category of fearful-avoidant represents high avoidance and high anxiety (see Figure 4).

The validity of conceptualizing attachment in this way has been demonstrated empirically, at least to some degree. For example, Fraley and Waller (1998) found that attachment relationships in adulthood cannot be easily demarcated from one another and therefore it may be more accurate to use continuous rather than discrete measures.

As an example of a more complex self-report measure of attachment, the Experiences in Close Relationships-Revised (ECR-R) questionnaire contains 36 statements such as 'I worry about being abandoned', 'I find it difficult to allow myself to depend on romantic partners' and 'I get frustrated when my partner is not around as much as I would like'. When completing the measure (widely and freely available online), each of the 36 statements is rated on a seven-point Likert scale from 'strongly agree' to 'strongly disagree'. Eighteen of the statements relate to avoidance and 18 to anxiety. Scoring involves a calculation of the average score for avoidance statements and for anxiety statements.

The Experiences in Close Relationships-Relationship Structures (ECR-RS) questionnaire is based on the ECR but can be used to assess attachment-related avoidance and anxiety for several different

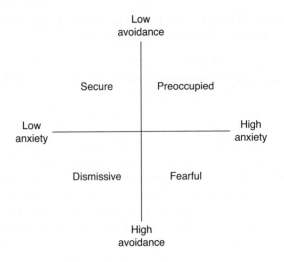

FIGURE 4   *A two-dimensional construct of adult attachment*

possible attachment figures. These individual, relationship-specific scores can then be averaged together in order to produce a global attachment score. The ECR-RS uses the following nine statements:

1. It helps to turn to this person in times of need.
2. I usually discuss my problems and concerns with this person.
3. I talk things over with this person.
4. I find it easy to depend on this person.
5. I don't feel comfortable opening up to this person.
6. I prefer not to show this person how I feel deep down.
7. I often worry that this person doesn't really care for me.
8. I'm afraid this person may abandon me.
9. I worry that this person won't care about me as much as I care about him or her.

As with the ECR, each statement in the ECR-RS is scored on a seven-point Likert scale from 'strongly agree' to 'strongly disagree'. An avoidance score is calculated by taking the average score for items one to six ('reverse scoring' items one, two, three and four[1]) and an anxiety score is calculated by taking the average score for items seven to nine. These scores can be calculated separately for each relationship and a general score calculated from the average of these.

When using any self-report measure of attachment, it is important to consider whether the measure has construct validity, that is, the extent to which it measures what it claims to measure, and to what degree. For example, Fairchild and Finney (2006) found that the Experiences in Close Relationships-Revised (ECR-R) questionnaire does have a reasonable degree of validity, although they also found that some of the statements may be extraneous (i.e. they are unrelated to the subject being studied or measured).

KEY TEXTS

- Brennan, K. A., Clark, C. L. and Shaver, P. (1998) 'Self-report Measurement of Adult Romantic Attachment: An Integrative Overview' in J. A. Simpson and W. S. Rholes (eds), *Attachment Theory and Close Relationships* (New York: Guilford Press): pp. 46–76
- Griffin, D. and Bartholomew, K. (1994b) 'Models of the Self and Other: Fundamental Dimensions Underlying Measures of Adult Attachment', *Journal of Personality and Social Psychology*, 67 (3): pp. 430–445
- Jacobvitz, D., Curran, M. and Moller, N. (2002) Measure of Adult Attachment: The Place of Self-report and Interview Methodologies', *Attachment and Human Development*, 4 (2): pp. 207–215

NOTE

1. Reverse scoring simply means turning the scale around, so that a 1 is treated as a 6 (and 2 as a 5, 3 as a 4) for the purposes of the calculation of the average.

separation protest

SEE ALSO **attunement and sensitivity; goal-oriented behaviour; insecure attachment; proximity-seeking and safe-haven behaviours**

Separation protest refers to the anxious response of infants when separated from their attachment figures and is widely accepted as being a normal part of child development. One of the primary aims of separation protest is to maintain proximity with an attachment figure and to prompt the attachment figure to demonstrate caregiving behaviour. Therefore, infant behaviour indicative of separation protest – such as crying, calling out and following – can be thought of as a form of *goal-oriented behaviour,* aimed at prompting the attachment figure to end the separation which in turn tends to end the display of separation protest by the infant. The behavioural display of separation protest usually begins at around 6 months of age, peaking and then declining at around 12 months of age. It may also return around the time the child is two years of age for a relatively brief period. Thus, separation protest occurs alongside the formation of the infant's attachment relationships and although the infant's experience of separation anxiety is not significantly influenced by the child's attachment relationships per se, the nature of the infant's separation-anxiety-related behaviour is influenced by the attachment figure's responses to it. For example, infants with *avoidant attachment* relationships will tend to minimize their display of separation protest compared with infants with *secure attachment* relationships. In contrast, infants with ambivalent-resistant relationships will tend to exaggerate their display of separation protest.

Whilst separation protest as a discrete phase of development is thought to occur universally, an individual's sense of anxiety about being abandoned remains central to attachment theory as applied across the lifespan, including in *later life attachments.* For example, in *self-report measures of attachment,* it is common to ask respondents to consider statements such as 'I don't often worry about being abandoned', with some adults, those with secure attachment states of mind, tending to agree and other adults, those with *insecure attachment* states of mind, tending to disagree.

KEY TEXTS
- Bowlby, J. (1960) 'Separation Anxiety', *The International Journal of Psychoanalysis,* 41: pp. 89–113
- Kobak, R. and Madsen, S. (2008) 'Disruptions in Attachment Bonds: Implications for Theory, Research, and Clinical Interventions' in J. Cassidy and P. Shaver (eds), *Handbook of Attachment: Theory, Research and Clinical Implications.* 2nd edn (London: Guilford Press)

Story Stem Completion

SEE ALSO **internal working models; measures of attachment**

Story Stem Completion provides the basis for a number of *measures of attachment,* typically used to assess the *internal working models* of children in middle childhood (between four and eight years of age, although some such measures can be used with older or younger children as well). Examples include the MacArthur Story Stem Battery, the Attachment Story Completion Test, the Story Stem Assessment Profile, the Attachment Doll Play Assessment, the Manchester Child Attachment Story Task and the Attachment Story Completion Task.

Although each of these methods is different, they all share a basic common technique. For any of these methods, the child is told the beginning – or stem – of a number of different stories that will mildly activate the child's attachment system and is then asked to continue and complete the story in whichever way they choose. The child is not asked any direct questions; neither are they asked to 'act out' any situations they themselves may have experienced (at least, not purposefully). Many of these measures involve the use of props, such as toy figures, with which the child is invited to 'show and tell' the story. The following is an example of the kind of stem used in these measures:

> Mum and dad and their two children are getting ready to go out. Just before they go, mum says to dad 'have you got the keys?'
> Dad says 'No, I haven't got them. I thought you had them!'
> Mum says 'Well, I haven't got them' (see Appleman and Palmer Wolf, 2003).

These stems tend to be based on situations that could involve 'separation anxiety', *loss and bereavement*, domestic arguments, fear and danger. In other words, the stems are designed to induce a mild level of stress in the child and as such, these methods are designed to replicate the experience of an infant within the *Strange Situation Procedure*. The theoretical assumption of these measures is that if children routinely experience a particular kind of care from their attachment figures, then these experiences become 'taken-for-granted' in their understanding of close relationships (see Crittenden, 1994); in other words, they will form part of the child's internal working model of attachment.

In addition, these measures usually require the child to be recorded as they respond to the stems, in order that the child's responses can be properly analysed by a trained coder. For example, many of these measures include a consideration of whether the child addressed the attachment-related issue presented in the stem. A consistent 'failure' to do so may lead to an overall judgement of the child as having experienced *avoidant attachment* relationships. More specifically, the Story Stem Assessment Profile uses a coding system based on the quality of the child's engagement, any disorganization or aggression within the stories, the representation of children and adults, and evidence of positive adaptations to the circumstances of the stem. However, caution is required when analysing and assessing a child's responses as all of these measures are deliberately precise. Thus, it is only the content of the child's stories within a properly conducted and validated measure that should be analysed by a suitably trained coder and not, for example, any stories the child may tell in otherwise free play.

With regards to *child maltreatment* or *neglected children*, there is a relatively substantial body of research to suggest that these children's stories are more likely to contain themes of aggression, violence and negative representations of attachment figures. The stories told by these children are also more likely to represent adults failing to respond to the child's distress or failing to offer help to the child. Some children who have been maltreated or seriously neglected may also tell stories with bizarre or catastrophic content, such as a mild family disagreement escalating into unresolved violence, and even murder. Hodges *et al.* (2003) used the Story Stem Assessment Profile with a group of adopted children, some of whom were adopted as infants and some of whom were adopted later in life, having experienced child maltreatment. They found that the children who were adopted as infants told relatively 'normal' stories, in the sense of being 'in keeping' with the stories of most non-maltreated children. However, children in the other group, those who were placed for adoption later in life and who had previously been maltreated, initially told stories that contained elements of fear, extreme aggression, catastrophes and disorganization. When the same group of children were asked to complete the Story Stem Assessment Profile one year later, this second set of story stems revealed an increase in positive internal working models but, interestingly, no apparent decrease in negative internal working models. As noted by Hodges *et al.*, this suggests that whilst these children were adapting to the (more sensitive and responsive) behaviour of their adoptive carers, they still carried

with them some important 'imprints' of their previous, more difficult experiences.

Some of these data – and the measures used to collect them – are
contested, at least to some degree, and as with many such research
tools, further validation work is needed both to correlate story stem
approaches with other measures of attachment and to ensure they
measure what they claim to measure (i.e. attachment).

KEY TEXTS

- Green, J., Stanley, C., Smith, V. and Goldwyn, R. (2000) 'A New
  Method of Evaluating Attachment Representations in Young School-
  Age Children: The Manchester Child Attachment Story Task',
  Attachment and Human Development, 2 (1): pp. 48–70
- Hodges, M., Hillman, S., Henderson, K. and Kaniuk, J. (2003)
  'Changes in Attachment Representations over the First Year of
  Adoptive Placement: Narratives of Maltreated Children', *Clinical Child
  Psychology and Psychiatry*, 8 (3): pp. 1359–1045
- Steele, M., Steele, H., Woolgar, M., Yabsley, S., Fonagy, P., Johnson,
  D. and Croft, C. (2003) 'An Attachment Perspective on Children's
  Emotion Narratives: Links across Generations' in R. Emde, D. Wolf and
  D. Oppenheim (eds), *Revealing the Inner Worlds of Young Children: The
  MacArthur Story Stem Battery and Parent–Child Narratives* (New York:
  Oxford University Press): pp. 163–181

Strange Situation Procedure

SEE ALSO **history of attachment theory and research; internal working
models; measures of attachment**

The significance of a child's reactions to strange situations (in the
colloquial meaning) and the variables that might help or hinder a
child's adjustment when faced with anxiety-inducing circumstances
has long been recognized within psychological research. Certainly
it was recognized at least two decades before Mary Ainsworth
devised the *Strange Situation Procedure* in the late 1960s as a way of
investigating the attachment relationships of infants. For example,
Shirley (1942) considered the adjustment of 'non-problem' children to a 'relatively novel situation' and reported that the child's
level of adjustment appeared to depend upon the 'wholesomeness
of his upbringing in the home, and the security and confidence and

affection given him by his parents'. Although referring to 'whole-someness' will no doubt strike modern sensibilities as unwarranted and value-laden, the references in the second half of the sentence, to the security, confidence and affection of his (or her) parents, are remarkably prescient of a great deal of subsequent attachment-based research. Thus, although the Strange Situation Procedure is one of the most widely used and robust *measures of attachment*, upon its inception it did not necessarily represent a completely new method for understanding or investigating the nature and quality of various elements of child development. A further example of this can be found in 1968, ten years before Ainsworth and colleagues published their seminal work regarding the Strange Situation Procedure, when Cox and Campbell published a paper regarding two experiments in which children were placed into 'new situations' and observed playing with or without their *mothers*. Cox and Campbell noted how the children tended to demonstrate less speech, movement and play when their mothers were absent and more when they were present. In attachment research, similar observations would lead to the development of the idea of the *secure base* and of the relationship between *exploration and security*.

What the Strange Situation Procedure did very successfully was to offer a standardized method for the assessment of the infant's behaviour towards his or her attachment figures at times of separation and reunion in particular. Specifically, Ainsworth and her colleagues developed the Strange Situation Procedure in order to try and understand three particular kinds of behaviour: i) the use of the attachment figure as a secure base from which to explore, ii) *separation protest* by the child and iii) the response when encountering a stranger (1978, p. viii). Ainsworth first formally observed these kinds of behaviour during her study of Ugandan infants but when she subsequently observed American infants in their homes, these behaviours emerged less clearly and so the Strange Situation Procedure was devised as a way of inducing them. As described by Ainsworth and colleagues, the Strange Situation Procedure takes place as follows:

> The (child), accompanied by his mother, was introduced to an unfamiliar but otherwise un-alarming playroom where massive instigation to exploratory behavior was provided by a large array

of toys. In the next episode, an adult stranger entered, who was tactful but nevertheless unfamiliar. Then came a brief separation episode in which the mother left the baby with the stranger. Then after an episode of reunion with the mother, there was a second separation in which the baby was first alone in the unfamiliar environment and then again with the stranger, who returned before the mother reentered. Because it was anticipated that experience in each episode would affect behavior in the next episode, the instigation to attachment behavior expected to be the weakest was placed at the beginning and that expected to be strongest toward the end. The expectations that these mild instigations would be cumulative in their effect were fulfilled. (1978, p. xi)

Early studies based on the Strange Situation Procedure showed that different patterns of infant behaviour could be understood as representing three distinctive ways of organizing the infant–adult attachment relationship – these would later become known as the familiar infant patterns of *secure attachment, ambivalent-resistant attachment* and *avoidant attachment*. Ainsworth and colleagues found that most of the children they studied had secure attachment relationships, with a smaller number having avoidant attachment relationships and even smaller numbers having ambivalent-resistant attachment relationships. As the popularity and reputation of the Strange Situation Procedure grew, researchers used the method with children from a variety of different countries and cultures and there initially developed a consensus that large *cultural differences* would exist between these children in terms of the distribution of the three infant attachment patterns. However, in 1988, van IJzendoorn and Kroonenberg systematically examined the available data and concluded that inter-cultural differences were more significant than cross-cultural differences. For example, van IJzendoorn and Kroonenberg found that for some samples of children, the distribution of these attachment patterns were more similar between areas of the United States, Israel, the Netherlands and Japan than between different areas of the United States. These data may indicate that a child's local circumstances – their immediate caregiving environment – may have a more significant impact on their display of attachment behaviour than wider cultural factors. As with many other *measures of attachment,* in order to use the Strange Situation Procedure properly, one should be fully trained and validated in one's coding ability.

KEY TEXTS

- Ainsworth, M., Blehar, M., Waters, E. and Wall, S. (1978) *Patterns of Attachment: A Psychological Study of the Strange Situation* (Hillsdale, New Jersey: Lawrence Erlbaum Associates)
- van IJzendoorn, M. and Kroonenberg, P. (1988) 'Cross-cultural Patterns of Attachment: A Meta-analysis of the Strange Situation', *Child Development,* 59 (1): pp. 147–156

t

temperament

SEE ALSO **genetic influences**

Which of the following statements, if any, relate to the child's attachment relationships?

1. Child is careful and gentle with toys and pets.
2. Child is more interested in people than things.
3. Child laughs and smiles easily with a lot of different people.
4. Child quickly gets used to people or things that initially made her/him shy or frightened.
5. Child prefers toys that are modelled after living things.

And which of these statements, if any, relate to the child's attachment relationships?

1. Child readily shares with carer or lets her/him hold things if she asks.
2. When child is near carer and sees something s/he wants to play with, s/he doesn't fuss or try to drag her/him over to it.
3. Child is willing to talk to new people, show them toys or show them what s/he can do, if the carer asks them to.
4. Child enjoys relaxing in carer's lap.
5. Child clearly shows a pattern of using the carer as a base from which to explore.
6. Child recognizes when carer is upset and becomes quiet and upset her/himself.

Temperament refers to innate elements of personality, rather than those learned through experience, imitation or modelling. Although there is no consensus on exactly what elements of our personalities are in fact innate, various suggestions have been made – including adaptability, introversion or extroversion, distractibility, mood and sensitivity. One of the better-known and most well-evidenced models of human personality is known as the 'Big Five' or OCEAN, incorporating five non-overlapping domains of personality – openness to experience, conscientiousness, extraversion, agreeableness and neuroticism. Openness to experience relates to the appreciation of novelty and variety or the display of curiosity about new things. Thus, people with less openness to experience will tend to prefer routine and familiarity. Conscientiousness relates to self-discipline and the control of impulses. People with less conscientiousness will therefore tend to act more impulsively. Extraversion relates to a person's breadth of activity and pronounced engagement and so people with less extraversion (or more introversion) will tend to engage in a narrower range of activities and with less 'energy'. Agreeableness relates to compassion and cooperation and hence people with less agreeable personalities will tend to be more competitive with others. Finally, neuroticism relates to the experience of negative emotions (such as sadness and fear) and can appear as emotional instability or a low threshold of tolerance for stress and anxiety.

Various research studies have shown that whilst these characteristics can vary over time – for example, changing with age –studies with identical twins have estimated the heritability of these characteristics as follows – openness to experience – 57 per cent; conscientiousness – 49 per cent; extraversion – 54 per cent; agreeableness – 42 per cent and neuroticism – 48 per cent. These data seem to suggest that genetic influences on these characteristics could be significant although of course many *nature and nurture arguments* are far from straightforward.

Thus, one pertinent research question is whether and to what degree attachment relationships might be influenced by temperament, as opposed to environmental factors, such as the behaviour of the child's attachment figures. Overall, it appears that the influence of temperamental characteristics on attachment relationships is modest. For example, various studies have estimated the influence of temperament on the variance between the attachment relationships of identical twins as being between approximately 10 and 25 per cent. Further evidence in regards to this question can be found in studies on whether infants may have different attachment relationships with different attachment figures. For example, the child may have a different kind of attachment relationship with two different primary carers (e.g. a *secure attachment* relationship with the mother and an *insecure attachment* relationship with the father). More recently, Vaughn, Bost and van IJzendoorn (2008) reviewed the state of attachment and temperament research and concluded that whilst temperamental differences may 'set the scene' for the child's attachment relationships, it is nevertheless the behaviour of the child's attachment figures, in response to both the temperament and other aspects of the child, that primarily determines the nature and quality of those attachment bonds. But these results may change when the age of the child is taken into account, as recent research by Fearon *et al.* (2014) shows a greater contribution from genes towards the organization of attachment responses as the child gets older. Although heritability contributes almost nothing to attachment in babies and toddlers, by mid-adolescence this recent study showed that genes might well account for around 50 per cent of the variation in attachment organization.

In relation to the statements at the start of this section, none of the first set relate to the child's attachment relationships and all of the second set do, especially statement number 5. The first set of statements most likely relate to the child's temperament.

KEY TEXTS

- Belsky, J. and Rovine, M. (1987) 'Temperament and Attachment Security in the Strange Situation: An Empirical Rapprochement', *Child Development*, 58 (3): pp. 787–795
- Fearon, P., Shmueli-Goetz, Y., Viding, E., Fonagy, P. and Plomin, R. (2014) 'Genetic and Environmental Influences on Adolescent Attachment', *Journal of Child Psychology and Psychiatry*, 55 (9) (September): pp. 1033–1041
- Vaughn, B., Bost, K. and van IJzendoorn, M. (2008) 'Attachment and Temperament: Additive and Interactive Influences on Behavior, Affect, and Cognition During Infancy and Childhood' in J. Cassidy and P. Shaver (eds), *The Handbook of Attachment: Theory, Research and Clinical Applications*. 2nd edn (New York: Guilford Press): pp. 192–216

theory of mind

SEE ALSO attunement and sensitivity; mentalization and reflective function; zero empathy

To possess a theory of mind is to ascribe mental states to oneself and to others and with regards to others, to make predictions about their behaviour based on these supposed mental states. Philosophically speaking, we can only hypothesize that other people (and perhaps some other animals) have a mind that operates at least a bit like our own because we have no direct evidence of whether they do or not. At times, we may also act as if certain non-living or inanimate objects have minds or at least that they have some attributes of a mind, such as intentionality. The philosopher Daniel Dennett refers to this as 'taking the intentional stance', that is, assuming that certain 'objects' (including people and animals) have intentions and using our assumptions about these intentions to predict future behaviour.[1] For example, if we imagine that a child really wants to retrieve their lost ball, we might be able to guess they are about to run across the road and thus be in a position to prevent them from doing so.

Research into how and at what age children develop a theory of mind has consistently found that younger children tend to demonstrate less well-developed theories of mind than older children, with something developmentally important taking place at around four years of age. One of the tests for theory of mind is known as the 'Sally–Anne' test (Wimmer and Perner, 1983). In this test, the child is introduced to two dolls, Sally and Anne, and the researcher then acts out the following story – Sally takes a marble and hides it in her basket. Sally then leaves the room. Whilst she is away, Anne takes the marble from Sally's basket and puts it in her own basket. Sally then returns to the room. At this point, the child is asked 'Where will Sally look for her marble'? (Baron-Cohen, Leslie and Frith, 1985). If the child answers 'correctly' – that Sally will look in her own basket – this is interpreted as demonstrating that the child has a theory of mind because they have shown an understanding that Sally has a different perspective from their own (i.e. Sally is in possession of less information than the child and the information Sally has will lead her to look in her own basket). On the other hand, if the child answers 'incorrectly' – that Sally will look in Anne's basket – this is interpreted as demonstrating that the child has not (fully) developed a theory of mind because they have (acted as if they) assumed Sally shares their knowledge as to the whereabouts of the marble (see Wellman, Cross and Watson, 2001). Several studies have found that children with certain developmental disorders, such as autism, are also more likely to 'fail' the test, even when they are older than four years of age. This has led many to conclude that most children develop a theory of mind at around four years of age, whilst also acknowledging that some children either do not develop a theory of mind or do so later than most other children (these ideas have been popularized in the bestselling novel, and now stage play, 'The Curious Incident of the Dog in the Night-Time', by Mark Haddon).

The ways in which children develop a theory of mind is interesting from an attachment perspective because they centre upon questions of whether and how early relational experiences might contribute. Indeed, it was more than 50 years ago that *Bowlby* argued that the nature of a child's attachment relationships shapes not only how they perceive other people but how they perceive themselves, via their *internal working models* of relationships. Children with *secure attachment* relationships are thought to form more coherent mental representations of their attachment figures and to more reliably predict what they might be thinking and feeling and what they might do. This enables the child in turn to more effectively adapt his or her own attachment behaviour. This process appears to share at least some similarities with the development of a theory of mind and it has been suggested that the experience of – in particular – early secure attachment relationships offers the child a 'forgiving space' in which to develop and practice their theory of mind-related abilities, ably assisted by one or more attachment figures.

However, the evidence in support of a link between attachment security and the development of a theory of mind is somewhat mixed, with various studies finding an association and other studies not. For example, Ontai and Thompson (2008) found that attachment security was not a predictor of theory of mind, and that knowing whether a child has an *insecure attachment* relationship or a secure attachment relationship does not enable one to predict whether the child will have a more or less developed theory of mind. Instead, Ontai and Thompson found that (maternal) 'elaborative discourse', which could include reflecting on the child's perceptions of events in contrast to other people's perceptions, or talking with the child about other people's feelings, thoughts, intentions, may be 'an important avenue by which young children derive an appreciation of mental states and their influence on behaviour' (p. 56).

Thus, whilst attachment security may not be predictive of the development of theory of mind in young children, it may be that some of the same *parenting* behaviours that make it more likely a child will develop a secure attachment relationship are also related to the child's more or less well-developed theory of mind.

KEY TEXTS

- Dennett, D. (1989) *The Intentional Stance* (Massachusetts: MIT University Press)
- Ontai, L. and Thompson, A. (2008) 'Attachment, Parent–Child Discourse and Theory-of-Mind Development', *Social Development*, 17 (1): pp. 47–60
- Wellman, H., Cross, D. and Watson, J. (2001) 'Meta-analysis of Theory-of-Mind Development: The Truth about False Belief', *Journal of Child Development*, 72 (3): pp. 655–684

NOTE

1. Although Dennet himself has argued that the phrase theory of mind is misleading, as the process or phenomenon being referred to is more akin to a craft than the kind of activity that would necessitate a theory to perform.

trans-generational transmission

SEE ALSO **Adult Attachment Interview; attunement and sensitivity; genetic influences; mentalization and reflective function; Strange Situation Procedure**

One of the key questions in attachment theory is how attachment patterns might be 'transmitted' from one generation to the next, from adult to child over time. In essence, the basic model suggested by attachment theory is this: children with *secure attachment* relationships are more likely to grow into adults with secure representations of attachment. These adults are in turn liable to create caregiving environments in which children are likely to develop

secure attachment relationships. Thus, secure patterns of attachment may be 'passed down' from generation to generation, from
adult to child, with the same being true for *insecure attachment*
patterns.

The development of the *Adult Attachment Interview* in the mid-
1980s gave researchers a way of comparing the attachment representations of adults with the behaviour of children in the *Strange
Situation Procedure* and as expected, there is a correlation between
children rated as secure in the latter and attachment figures rated
as secure in the former (indeed, the Adult Attachment Interview
was initially developed as a way of predicting the behaviour of children in the Strange Situation Procedure). Interestingly, this association is stronger when considering *mothers* as attachment figures
when compared with *fathers*, although this changes to some extent
in situations where the father is the child's primary carer (Bernier
and Miljkovitch, 2009). However, whilst these data may seem to
support the hypothesis that attachment patterns are transmitted
from adult to child, from one generation to the next, via the attachment representations of the adult, it is important to note two things:
firstly, these results do not address the question as to 'how' attachment patterns are transmitted from one generation to the next;
and secondly, one would expect to see similar results if attachment
security and insecurity were transmitted via genetic factors rather
than environmental ones (and the recent twins study by Pasco
Fearon published in September 2014 suggests this may be the case
through and beyond adolescence).

Therefore, this correlation – between children rated as secure
in the Strange Situation Procedure and adults rated as secure in
the Adult Attachment Interview – does not preclude the possibility
of *genetic influences* on attachment and neither does it confirm the
validity of the behavioural and mental representation hypothesis
as suggested by attachment theory. Thus, there has been a great
deal of further research undertaken with the aim of discovering
and understanding the various possible explanatory factors for this
correlation.

Mary Ainsworth, a close colleague of John *Bowlby*, initially
proposed that the sensitivity of the attachment figure towards the
child would be a key mediating factor in the intergenerational
transmission of attachment patterns. Ainsworth argued that if the

attachment figure responded in a reliably sensitive way to the child, the child would develop *internal working models* of the relationship as dependable and safe and would in turn develop a secure attachment relationship. Ainsworth further suggested that such children would grow into sensitive attachment figures themselves, thus perpetuating the transmission relationship. However, in a meta-analysis of the available data, Bakermans-Kranenburg, van IJzendoorn and Juffer (2003) found that although sensitivity is important, it is only modestly associated with infant attachment. Furthermore, the relationship between the two is one of association rather than causation. Later studies have suggested that maternal sensitivity is a significant mediating factor in the intergenerational transmission of attachment but only in certain situations (Tarabulsy *et al.*, 2005). These apparently conflicting results suggest that the relationship between the attachment figure's sensitivity and the child's attachment relationships is affected by the presence of other confounding or mediating variables so that sensitivity is more or less significant depending on the presence or absence of other factors.

Aside from the *attunement and sensitivity* of the attachment figure, one potentially significant factor within the intergenerational transmission of attachment is that of mentalization, known in the context of attachment as reflective functioning. These abilities – *mentalization and reflective function* – have been defined as 'the capacity to envision mental states in (the) self and others' (Fonagy and Target, 1999, p. 679). Fonagy and Target also note that 'Individuals differ in the extent to which they can go beyond observable phenomena to explain their own and others' actions in terms of belief, desires, plans, and so on' (p. 680) and that the relationship between mentalization and attachment security (or insecurity) may be located in the ability of the attachment figure to understand their child's behaviour in terms of underlying mental states and by so doing, to provide a model or 'scaffold' for the child to develop their own ability. Children are more likely to have secure attachment relationships when both the child and the attachment figure demonstrate consistently high levels of reflective functioning and this has led Fonagy and Target to suggest that the secure infant becomes [the] mentalizing child' (1999, p. 687). In turn, the mentalizing child may become the mentalizing attachment figure.

KEY TEXTS

- Bakermans-Kranenburg, M., van IJzendoorn, M. and Juffer, F. (2003) 'Less Is More: Meta-analyses of Sensitivity and Attachment Interventions in Childhood', *Psychological Bulletin*, 129 (2): pp. 195–215
- Fonagy, P. and Target, M. (1999) 'Attachment and Reflective Function: Their Role in Self-organization', *Development and Psychopathology*, 9 (4): pp. 679–700
- van IJzendoorn, M., Bakermans-Kranenburg, M. and Marian, J. (1997) 'Intergenerational Transmission of Attachment: A Move to the Contextual Level' in L. Atkinson and K. Zucker (eds), *Attachment and Psychopathology* (New York: Guilford Press): pp. 135–170

u

unresolved loss and trauma

SEE ALSO attunement and sensitivity; child maltreatment; disorganized attachment; dissociation; neglected children

When a physical injury is sustained, for example, a broken leg or fractured skull, it may be described as a trauma (to the body). Similarly, an emotional shock, especially one that has a lasting effect, may also be described as a trauma. In the United States, and possibly in the United Kingdom as well, it is considered, at least by some, that 'childhood trauma including abuse and neglect is probably the single most important public health challenge' (Benamer and White, 2008, p. 45). However, although trauma can be caused by events other than abuse or neglect, there may be an important difference in the subjective experience of trauma when it is caused by the actions (or inactions) of a person who is meant to care for, protect and nurture us. Emotional neglect and abuse by an attachment figure, for example, may be far more traumatic than even very catastrophic physical events.

Clearly, though, not all experiences of trauma are the same. In many cases, traumatic events may be 'resolved', meaning the memory of the trauma begins to make more sense in the present. However, in some cases, the trauma is 'unresolved', so that the memory stays locked in the past. A traumatic *memory* may be reactivated by sights, smells or sounds that remind the person of the original events (Fearon and Mansell, 2001). This sense of unresolved trauma, which may also apply to unresolved feelings of loss regarding a loved one, may be described as 'repeating what we can't remember' – what Prophecy Coles (2011) called 'The Uninvited Guest from the Unremembered Past', suggesting that we cannot control unresolved loss and trauma; instead it controls us, in the sense that memories return unannounced and usually unwanted.

The *Adult Attachment Interview* aims to help reveal whether an individual has unresolved experiences of loss and trauma. For example, Ainsworth and Eichberg (1991) describe one mother in particular who, during an Adult Attachment Interview, recalled an incident that happened during her childhood. A workman at her house had teased her by saying he would 'marry her when she got older'. She replied to him, in an innocent, child-like manner, that 'she couldn't do that, as he'd be dead'. Tragically, the workman died soon afterwards and in the Adult Attachment Interview, the mother stopped abruptly and, in an affected little girl's voice, said she 'had killed him with one sentence' (1991, p. 175). The manner in which this story was told suggests that the memory of being a little girl in that situation had intruded upon the mother during the interview, even after all the intervening years, and that somehow the mother had 'relived' the experience, however briefly.

As another example of how unresolved loss or trauma may be experienced, in the United Kingdom in 1985, there was a fire at the Bradford City football stadium, killing 56 people and injuring more than 265. Some weeks later, a number of the survivors reported feeling disoriented, sweating profusely and even losing consciousness. When they were asked what had been happening prior to these experiences, a number described hearing a particular sound, such as a packet of crisps being opened. A fire fighter who had been present recognized that this sound was similar to that of burning corrugated iron, the same material as found on the roof of the main stand. Thus it was suggested that hearing this sound had triggered painful and unresolved memories in some of the survivors and led to their experience of what we might now recognize as the symptoms of post-traumatic stress disorder.

KEY TEXTS

- Benamer, S. and White, K. (2008) *Trauma and Attachment* (London: Karnac Books)
- Lyons-Ruth, K., Yellin, C., Melnick, S. and Atwood, G. (2003) 'Childhood Experiences of Trauma and Loss Have Different Relations to Maternal Unresolved and Hostile-Helpless States of Mind on the AAI', *Attachment and Human Development*, 5 (4): pp. 330–414
- Walker, J. (2008) 'Guide to Unresolved Trauma in Parents and its Implications in Terms of Child Protection', *Community Care Inform.* http://www.ccinform.co.uk/guides/guide-to-unresolved-trauma-in-parents-and-its-implications-in-terms-of-child-protection/

V

Video-based Intervention to Promote Positive Parenting

SEE ALSO **attunement and sensitivity; interventions**

One of the more long-standing debates regarding attachment theory is whether and how the knowledge and expertise obtained from attachment-related research might be applied in clinical practice. In 2003, a group of researchers from the Center for Child and Family Studies at Leiden University undertook a meta-analysis in order to try and understand what kind of interventions had been more or less effective. They found that, overall, the more effective interventions were those based on a small to moderate number of sessions (fewer than 16) and which focused on observable behaviour: hence the title of their paper 'Less Is More'. They also found that interventions that were more effective in enhancing the *attunement and sensitivity* of the attachment figure were the most effective in enhancing the attachment security of the child (an experimental finding which supports the hypothesis that sensitivity has a causal role in shaping attachment security).

One intervention found to be particularly useful was the Video-based Intervention to Promote Positive Parenting (VIPP). For the purposes of VIPP, adults and infants are video-recorded together on various occasions at home, such as at meal times or play times. These tapes are then reviewed and selected extracts are shown to the child's carer, especially any examples of positive interactions between the child and the adult. The aim of using positive video feedback is not only to help the adult develop their observational and empathic skills – to help them understand how to tell when their child is happy, contented, excited and so on – but also to help them develop their self-confidence that the child enjoys being with them. The aim is to positively reinforce the adult so that they want to spend more time engaged in sensitive interactions with the child. In each session, the adult is invited to consider their infant's *proximity-seeking and safe-haven behaviours* and the child's use of the adult as a *secure base*, as well as to think about what the child's facial expressions and pre-verbal communication might mean. On occasion, the adult will be invited to 'speak for the baby', to verbalize what they think might have been 'going on' in the mind of the child at the time the video was taken. The whole process usually takes between four and eight sessions. Using VIPP over more than eight sessions does not appear to make the intervention any more effective and, in some cases, undertaking a greater number of sessions actually results in the intervention being less successful. Using randomized controlled trials (a method often referred to as the 'gold standard' of scientific research), VIPP has been found to be reasonably effective with children aged under five and for children in adoptive care although Berlin, Zeanah and Lieberman (2008) have also reported on some less successful uses of the method.

KEY TEXTS

- Bakermans-Kranenburg, M., van IJzendoorn, M. and Juffer, F. (2003) 'Less Is More: Meta-analyses of Sensitivity and Attachment Interventions in Early Childhood', *Psychological Bulletin*, 129 (2): pp. 195–215
- Berlin, L., Zeanah, B. and Lieberman, A. (2008) 'Prevention and Intervention Programs for Supporting Early Attachment Security' in J. Cassidy and P. Shaver (eds), *Handbook of Attachment: Theory, Research and Clinical Applications* (London: Guilford Press): pp. 749–750
- Juffer, F., Bakermans-Kranenburg, M. and van IJzendoorn, M. (2008) *Promoting Positive Parenting: An Attachment-based Intervention* (New York: Lawrence Erlbaum Associates)

Z

zero empathy

SEE ALSO **attunement and sensitivity**

Empathy is a key characteristic within attachment relationships, with higher levels of empathy being associated with *secure attachment* and lower levels of empathy with *insecure attachment*. Empathy is commonly defined as an ability to understand and share the feelings of others. However, Simon Baron-Cohen has defined empathy in more detail as follows:

> Empathy occurs when we suspend our single-minded focus of attention, and instead adopt a double-minded focus of attention. Empathy is our ability to identify what someone else is thinking or feeling, and to respond to their thoughts and feelings with an appropriate emotion. (p. 18, 2011)

Considering the *Strange Situation Procedure*, one can envision how more sensitive attachment figures are more able to identify, or even to predict, their infant's distress following a cycle of separation-and-reunion and to respond appropriately, not to how they might want the infant to feel or how they might be feeling themselves, but to how the infant is actually feeling, and thus to offer suitable comfort until the infant shows a desire to return to playing with the toys. Infants treated in this way are more likely to develop and maintain secure attachment relationships.

Not only may empathy have a bearing on the ability of the attachment figure to respond with sensitivity to the child, the development of the child's own empathetic abilities significantly occurs within the context of close attachment relationships. According to Baron-Cohen, empathy is not an innate quality, present from birth, but something that has to be nurtured, modelled and developed and that different people may develop different 'amounts of' empathy. It is also important to note Baron-Cohen's argument that having 'zero empathy' is not necessarily a negative and may not relate to the individual's relational experiences at all. However, in general terms, children who are 'empathized with' to a greater degree will tend to develop improved empathic abilities of their own whilst children who do not routinely experience empathic responses from others, particularly from their attachment figures, will tend to find it more difficult to display empathy themselves. Of course, many (potentially) short-term factors can also affect the expression of empathy as well, including stress, alcohol and fatigue. Thus, empathy is both something that has to be nurtured in order to develop but also something that waxes and wanes depending on more immediate circumstances.

KEY TEXTS

- Baron-Cohen, S. (2011) *Zero Degrees of Empathy* (London: Penguin)
- Coplan, A. and Goldie, P. (2011) *Empathy: Philosophical and Psychological Perspectives* (Oxford: Oxford University Press)
- Howe, D. (2008) *The Emotionally Intelligent Social Worker* (Basingstoke: Palgrave Macmillan)

bibliography

Aarts, H. and Elliot, J. (eds) (2012) *Goal-directed Behaviour* (New York: Psychology Press)

Ainsworth, M. (1969) 'Object Relations, Dependency, and Attachment: A Theoretical Review of the Infant–Mother Relationship', *Child Development*, 40 (4): pp. 969–1026

Ainsworth, M. and Bell, S. (1970) 'Attachment, Exploration, and Separation: Illustrated by the Behavior of One-Year-Olds in a Strange Situation', *Child Development*, 41 (4): pp. 49–67

Ainsworth, M., Blehar, M., Waters, E. and Wall, S. (1978) *Patterns of Attachment: A Psychological Study of the Strange Situation* (Hillsdale, NJ: Lawrence Erlbaum Associates)

Ainsworth, M. and Eichberg, C. (1991) 'Effects on Infant–Mother Attachment of Mother's Unresolved Loss of an Attachment Figure or Other Traumatic Experience' in P. Marris, C. Stevenson-Hinde and C. Parkes (eds), *Attachment across the Life Cycle* (New York: Routledge): pp. 160–183

Alexander, K., Quas, J. and Goodman, G. (2002) 'Theoretical Advances in Understanding Children's Memory for Distressing Events: The Role of Attachment', *Developmental Review*, 22 (3): pp. 490–519

Allen, J. and Miga, E. (2010) 'Attachment in Adolescence: A Move to the Level of Emotion Regulation', *Journal of Social and Personal Relationships*, 27 (2): pp. 181–190

Appelman, E. and Palmer Wolf, D. (2003) 'Emotional Apprenticeships: The Development of Affect Regulation during the Preschool Years' in R. Emde, D. Wolf and D. Oppenheim (eds), *Revealing the Inner Worlds of Young Children. The MacArthur Story Stem Battery and Parent–Child Narratives* (New York: Oxford University Press): pp. 182–198

Bakermans-Kranenburg, M. and van IJzendoorn, M. (2006) 'Gene–Environment Interaction of the Dopamine D4 Receptor (DRD4) and Observed Maternal Insensitivity Predicting Externalizing Behavior in Preschoolers', *Developmental Psychology*, 48 (5): pp. 406–409

Bakermans-Kranenburg, M. and van IJzendoorn, M. (2009) 'The First 10,000 Adult Attachment Interviews: Distributions of Adult Attachment Representations in Clinical and Non-clinical Groups', *Attachment and Human Development*, 11 (3): pp. 223–263

Bakermans-Kranenburg, M., van IJzendoorn, M. and Juffer, F. (2003) 'Less Is More: Meta-analyses of Sensitivity and Attachment Interventions in Early Childhood', *Psychological Bulletin*, 129 (2): pp. 195–215

Bargh, J. and Mosella, E. (2008) 'The Unconscious Mind', *Perspectives on Psychological Sciences*, 3 (1): pp. 73–79

Baron-Cohen, S. (2011) *Zero Degrees of Empathy* (London: Penguin)

Baron-Cohen, S., Leslie, A. and Frith, U. (1985) 'Does the Autistic Child Have a "Theory of Mind"?, *Journal of Cognition*, 21 (1): pp. 37–46

Barth, R., Crea, T., John, K., Thoburn, J. and Quinton, D. (2005) 'Beyond Attachment Theory and Therapy: Towards a Sensitive and Evidence-based Interventions with Foster and Adoptive Families in Distress', *Child and Family Social Work*, 10 (4): pp. 257–268

Bartholomew, K. (1990) 'Avoidant of Intimacy: An Attachment Perspective', *Journal of Social and Personal Relationships*, 7 (2): pp. 147–178

Bartholomew, K. and Moretti, M. (2002) 'The Dynamics of Measuring Attachment', *Attachment and Human Development*, 4 (2): pp. 162–165

Baumrind, D. (1967) 'Child Care Practices Anteceding Three Patterns of Preschool Behavior', *Genetic Psychology Monographs*, 75 (1): pp. 43–88

Beck, R. (2006) 'God as a Secure Base: Attachment to God and Theological Exploration', *Journal of Psychology and Theology*, 34 (2): pp. 125–132

Bell, D. (2012) *The Dynamics of Connection: How Evolution and Biology Create Caregiving and Attachment* (Plymouth, England: Lexington Books)

Belsky, J. (2009) 'Beyond Diathesis Stress: Differential Susceptibility to Environmental Influences', *Psychological Bulletin*, 135 (6): pp. 885–908

Belsky, J. and Pluess, M. (2009) 'Beyond Diathesis Stress: Differential Susceptibility to Environmental Influences', *Psychological Bulletin*, 135 (6): pp. 885–908

Belsky, J. and Rovine, M. (1987) 'Temperament and Attachment Security in the Strange Situation: An Empirical Rapprochement', *Child Development*, 58 (3): pp. 787–795

Benamer, S. and White, K. (2008) *Trauma and Attachment* (London: Karnac Books)

Benoit, D. and Parker, K. (1994) 'Stability and Transmission of Attachment across Three Generations', *Child Development*, 65 (5): pp. 1444–1456

Berlin, L., Zeanah, B. and Lieberman, A. (2008) 'Prevention and Intervention Programs for Supporting Early Attachment Security', in J. Cassidy and P. Shaver (eds), *Handbook of Attachment: Theory, Research and Clinical Applications*. (pp. 749–750). (London: Guilford Press): pp. 749–750

Bernard, K., Dozier, M., Bick, J., Lewis-Morrarty, E., Lindhiem, O. and Carlson, E. (2012) 'Enhancing Attachment Organization among Maltreated Children: Results of a Randomized Clinical Trial', *Child Development*, 83 (2): pp. 623–636

Bernier, A. and Miljkovitch, R. (2009) 'Intergenerational Transmission of Attachment in Father–Child Dyads: The Case of Single Parenthood', *The Journal of Genetic Psychology: Research and Theory on Human Development*, 170 (1): pp. 31–52

Bifulco, A. and Thomas, G. (2012) *Understanding Adult Attachment in Family Relationships: Research, Assessment and Intervention* (London: Routledge)

Bowlby, J. (1960) 'Separation Anxiety', *The International Journal of Psychoanalysis*, 41: pp. 89–113

Bowlby, J. (1969) *Attachment. Attachment and Loss, Volume 1: Loss* (New York: Basic Books)

Bowlby, J. (1980) *Attachment and Loss, Volume 3: Loss, Sadness and Depression* (New York: Basic Books)

Bowlby, J. (1991) *Charles Darwin: A New Life* (New York: W. W. Norton and Company)

Bowlby, J. (1997) *Attachment: Volume One of the Attachment and Loss Trilogy: Attachment Vol 1 (Attachment and Loss)*. Revised edn (Pimlico, London: Random House)

Bowlby, J. (2005) *A Secure Base*. Re-issue edn (London: Routledge)

Bowlby, J. and Parkes, C. M. (1970) 'Separation and Loss within the Family', in E. J. Anthony (ed.), *The Child in His family* (New York: J. Wiley)

Bremner, J. and Marmar, C. (eds) (1998) *Trauma, Memory and Dissociation* (Washington, DC: American Psychiatric Press)

Brennan, K. A., Clark, C. L. and Shaver, P. (1998) 'Self-report Measurement of Adult Romantic Attachment: An Integrative Overview', in J. A. Simpson and W. S. Rholes (eds), *Attachment Theory and Close Relationships* (New York: Guilford Press): pp. 46–76

Bretherton, I. (1985) 'Attachment Theory: Retrospect and Prospect', *Monographs of the Society for Research in Child Development*, 50 (1–2): pp. 3–35

Bretherton, I. (1992) 'The Origins of Attachment Theory: John Bowlby and Mary Ainsworth', *Developmental Psychology*, 28 (5): pp. 759–775

Bretherton, I. (2011) 'Fathers in Attachment Theory and Research: A Review', *Early Child Development and Care*, 180 (1–2): pp. 9–23

Bretherton, I. and Munholland, K. (2008) 'Internal Working Models in Attachment Relationships: Elaborating a Central Construct in Attachment Theory' in J. Cassidy and P. Shaver (eds), *Handbook of Attachment: Theory, Research and Clinical Applications*. 2nd edn (New York: Guilford Press): pp. 102–127

Brown, R. and Ward, H. (2012) 'Decision-making within a Child's Timeframe. An Overview of Current Research Evidence for Family Justice Professionals Concerning Child Development and the Impact of Maltreatment' (Childhood Wellbeing Research Centre). Available at https://www.gov.uk/government/uploads/system/uploads/attach-ment_data/file/200471/Decision-making_within_a_child_s_time-frame.pdf

Browne, C. and Shlosberg, E. (2006) 'Attachment Theory, Ageing and Dementia: A Review of the Literature', *Aging and Mental Health*, 10 (2): pp. 134–142

Byng-Hall, J. (2002) 'Relieving Parentified Children's Burdens in Families with Insecure Attachment Patterns', *Family Process*, 41 (3): pp. 375–388

Caron, A., Lafontaine, M., Bureau, J., Levesque, C. and Johnson, S. (2012) 'Comparisons of Close Relationships: An Evaluation of Relationship Quality and Patterns of Attachment to Parents, Friends, and Romantic Partners in Young Adults', *Canadian Journal of Behavioural Science*, 44 (4): pp. 245–256

Cassidy, J. and Berlin, L. (1994) 'The Insecure/Ambivalent Pattern of Attachment: Theory and Research', *Child Development*, 65 (4): pp. 971–991

Cassidy, J. and Shaver, P. (eds) (2008) *Handbook of Attachment: Theory, Research and Clinical Applications* (London: Guilford Press)

Cassidy, J., Woodhouse, S., Sherman, L., Stupica, B. and Lejuez, C. (2011) 'Enhancing Infant Attachment Security: An Examination of Treatment Efficacy and Differential Susceptibility', *Journal of Development and Psychopathology*, 23 (1): pp. 131–148

Chamberlain, P., Price, J., Reid, J., Landsverk, J., Fisher, P. and Stoolmiller, M. (2006) 'Who Disrupts from Placement in Foster and Kinship Care?', *Child Abuse and Neglect*, 30 (4): pp. 409–424

Chisholm, K. (1998) 'A Three-Year Follow-Up of Attachment and Indiscriminate Friendliness in Children Adopted from Romanian Orphanages', *Child Development*, 69 (4): pp. 1092–1106

Chopik, W., Edelstein, R. and Fraley, R. C. (2013) 'From the Cradle to the Grave: Age Differences in Attachment from Early Adulthood to Old Age', *Journal of Personality*, 81 (2): pp. 171–183

Cicchetti, D. and Carlson, V. (eds) (1989) *Child Maltreatment: Theory and Research on the Causes and Consequences of Child Abuse and Neglect* (Cambridge: Cambridge University Press)

Clulow, C. (ed.) (2001) *Adult Attachment and Couple Psychotherapy: The 'Secure Base' in Practice and Research* (London: Routledge)

Coles, P. (2011) *The Uninvited Guest from the Unremembered Past* (London: Karnac Books)

Collins, N., Feeney, B. and Brooke, C. (2000) 'A Safe Haven: An Attachment Theory Perspective on Support Seeking and Caregiving in Intimate

Relationships', *Journal of Personality and Social Psychology*, 78 (6): pp. 1053–1073

Coplan, A. and Goldie, P. (2011) *Empathy: Philosophical and Psychological Perspectives* (Oxford: Oxford University Press)

Cox, F. and Campbell, D. (1968) 'Young Children in a New Situation with and without Their Mothers', *Child Development*, 39 (1): pp. 123–131

Crittenden, P. (1994) 'Peering into the Black Box: An Exploratory Treatise on the Development of Self in Young Children' in P. Cichetti and S. Toth (eds), *Clinical Implications of Attachment* (Hillsdale, NJ: Elbaum): pp. 136–174

Crittenden, P. (2006) 'A Dynamic-Maturational Model of Attachment', *Australian and New Zealand Journal of Family Therapy*, 27 (2): pp. 105–115

Crittenden, P. (2008) *Raising Parents: Attachment Parenting and Child Safety* (London: Routledge)

Crowell, J. and Treboux, D. (1995) 'A Review of Adult Attachment Measures: Implications for Theory and Research', *Social Development*, 4: pp. 294–327

Cyr, C., Euser, E., Bakermans-Kranenberg, M. and van IJzendoorn, M. (2010) 'Attachment Security and Disorganisation in Maltreating and High-Risk Families: A Series of Meta-analyses', *Development and Psychopathology*, 22 (1): pp. 87–108

Davila, J. and Kashy, D. (2009) 'Secure Base Processes in Couples: Daily Associations between Support Experiences and Attachment Security', *Journal of Family Psychology*, 23 (1): pp. 76–88

De Wit, S. and Dickinson, A. (2009) 'Associative Theories of Goal-directed Behaviour: A Case for Animal–Human Translational Models', *Psychological Research*, 73 (4): pp. 463–476

Del Giudice, M. (2009) 'Sex, Attachment, and the Development of Reproductive Strategies', *Behavioral and Brain Sciences*, 32 (1): pp. 1–21

Dennett, D. (1996) *The Intentional Stance*. 6th edn (Cambridge, MA: MIT Press)

Doherty, N. and Feeney, J. (2004) 'The Composition of Attachment Networks throughout the Adult Years', *Journal of Personal Relationships*, 11 (4): pp. 469–488

Erich, S., Kanenberg, H., Case, K., Allen, T. and Bogdanos, T. (2009) 'An Empirical Analysis of Factors Affecting Adolescent Attachment in Adoptive Families with Homosexual and Straight Parents', *Children and Youth Services Review*, 31 (3): pp. 398–404

Fairchild, A. and Finney, S. (2006) 'Investigating Validity Evidence for the Experiences in Close Relationships-Revised Questionnaire', *Educational and Psychological Measurement*, 66 (1): pp. 116–135

Farnfield, S., Hautamaki, A., Norbech, P. and Sahhar, N. (2010) 'Dynamic-Maturational Model Assessments of Attachment and Adaptation', *Clinical Child Psychology and Psychiatry*, 15 (3): pp. 313–328

Fearon, R. and Mansell, W. (2001) 'Cognitive Perspectives on Unresolved Loss: Insights from the Study of PTSD', *Bulletin of the Menninger Clinic*, 65 (3): pp. 380–396

Fearon, P., Shmueli-Goetz, Y., Viding, E., Fonagy, P. and Plomin, R. (2014) 'Genetic and Environmental Influences on Adolescent Attachment', *Journal of Child Psychology and Psychiatry*, 55 (9) (September): pp. 1033–1041

Featherstone, B., White, S. and Morris, K. (2014) *Re-imagining Child Protection: Towards Humane Social Work with Families* (Bristol: Policy Press), Chapter 4

Feeney, B. and Collins, N. (2004) 'Interpersonal Safe Haven and Secure Base Caregiving Processes in Adulthood' in W. Rholes and J. Simpson (eds), *Adult Attachment: Theory, Research and Clinical Implications* (New York: Guilford Press): pp. 300–338

Flanagan, L. (2011) 'Object Relations Theory' in. J. Berzoff, L. Flanagan and P. Hertz (eds), *Inside Out and Outside In: Psychodynamic Clinical Theory and Psychopathology in Contemporary Multicultural Contexts.* 3rd edn (Maryland: Rowman and Littlefield Publishers): pp. 118–157

Fonagy, P., Bateman, A. and Bateman, A. (2011) 'The Widening Scope of Mentalization: A Discussion', *Psychology and Psychotherapy: Theory, Research and Practice*, 84 (1): pp. 98–110

Fonagy, P., Gergely, G., Jurist, E. and Target, M. (2004) *Affect Regulation, Mentalization, and the Development of the Self* (London: Karnac Books)

Fonagy, P., Steele, M., Moran, G., Steele, H. and Higgitt, A. (1991) 'The Capacity for Understanding Mental States: The Reflective Self in Parent and Child and Its Significance for Security of Attachment', *Infant Mental Health Journal*, 12 (3): pp. 201–218

Fonagy, P. and Target, M. (1999) 'Attachment and Reflective Function: Their Role in Self-organization', *Development and Psychopathology*, 9 (4): pp. 679–700

Fraley, R. C., Garner, J. and Shaver, P. (2000) 'Adult Attachment and the Defensive Regulation of Attention and Memory: Examining the Role of Pre-emptive and Post-emptive Defensive Processes', *Journal of Personality and Social Psychology*, 79 (5): pp. 816–826

Fraley, R. C., Niedenthal, P., Marks, M., Brumbaugh, C. and Vicary, A. (2006) 'Adult Attachment and the Perception of Emotional Expressions: Probing the Hyperactivating Strategies Underlying Anxious Attachment', *Journal of Personality*, 74 (4): pp. 1163–1190

Fraley, R. C., Vicary, A., Brumbaugh, C. and Roisman, G. (2011) 'Patterns of Stability in Adult Attachment: An Empirical Test of Two Models of Continuity and Change', *Journal of Personality and Social Psychology*, 101 (5): pp. 974–992

Fraley, R. C. and Waller, N. G. (1998) 'Adult Attachment Patterns: A Test of the Typological Model' in J. Simpson and W. Rhodes (eds), Attachment Theory and Close Relationships (New York: Guilford Press): pp. 77–114

Fraley, R. C., Waller, N. G. and Brennan, K. A. (2000) 'An Item-Response Theory Analysis of Self-report Measures of Adult Attachment', *Journal of Personality and Social Psychology*, 78 (2): pp. 350–365

Gao, Y., Raine, A., Chan, F., Venables, P. and Mednick, S. (2010) 'Early Maternal and Paternal Bonding, Childhood Physical Abuse and Adult Psychopathic Personality', *Psychological Medicine*, 40 (6): pp. 1007–1016

Gentzler, A. and Kerns, K. (2006) 'Adult Attachment and Memory of Emotional Reactions to Negative and Positive Events', *Journal of Cognition and Emotion*, 20 (1): pp. 20–42

George, C., Kaplan, N. and Main, M. (1996) *Adult Attachment Interview Protocol*. 3rd edn. Unpublished Manuscript, University of California at Berkley. Available at http://www.psychology.sunysb.edu/attachment/measures/content/aai_interview.pdf

Gervai, J. (2009) 'Environmental and Genetic Influences on Early Attachment', *Child and Adolescent Psychiatry and Mental Health*, 3 (25), doi: 10.1186/1753-2000-3-25

Golding, K. (2007) 'Developing a Group-based Parent Training for Foster and Adoptive Parents', *Adoption and Fostering*, 31 (3): pp. 39–48

Golding, K. (2014) 'Fostering Attachment Group Summary of Research'. Available at http://ddpnetwork.org/backend/wp-content/uploads/2014/01/Fostering-Attachment-Group-Summary-of-Research.-Kim-Golding-.pdf

Golombok, S. and Badger, S. (2010) 'Children Raised in Mother-headed Families from Infancy: A Follow-Up of Children of Lesbian and Single Heterosexual Mothers, at Early Adulthood', *Human Reproduction*, 25 (1): pp. 150–157

Green, J., Stanley, C., Smith, V. and Goldwyn, R. (2000) 'A New Method of Evaluating Attachment Representations in Young School-Age Children: The Manchester Child Attachment Story Task', *Attachment and Human Development*, 2 (1): pp. 48–70

Grice, P. (1975) 'Logic and Conversation' in P. Cole and J. Morgan (eds), *Syntax and Semantics* (New York: Academic Press): pp. 41–58

Griffin, D. and Bartholomew, K. (1994a) 'The Metaphysics of Measurement: The Case of Adult Attachment' in K. Bartholomew and D. Perlman (eds)

Attachment Processes in Adulthood (London: Jessica Kingsley Publishers): pp. 17–52

Griffin, D. and Bartholomew, K. (1994b) 'Models of the Self and Other: Fundamental Dimensions Underlying Measures of Adult Attachment', *Journal of Personality and Social Psychology*, 67 (3): pp. 430–445

Gross, J. (1999) 'Emotion Regulation: Past, Present and Future', *Cognition and Emotion*, 13 (5): pp. 551–573

Grossmann, K., Grossmann, K., Fremmer-Bombik, E., Kindler, H., Scheuerer-Englisch, H. and Zimmermann, P. (2002) 'The Uniqueness of the Child–Father Attachment Relationship: Fathers' Sensitive and Challenging Play as a Pivotal Variable in a 16-Year Longitudinal Study', *Social Development*, 11 (3): pp. 301–337

Harlow, H. and Zimmermann, R. (1959) 'Affectional Responses in the Infant Monkey', *Science*, 130: pp. 421–432

Hazan, C. and Shaver, P. (1987) 'Romantic Love Conceptualized as an Attachment Process', *Journal of Personality and Social Psychology*, 52 (3): pp. 511–524

Hesse, E. (2008) 'The Adult Attachment Interview' in J. Cassidy and P. Shaver (eds), *Handbook of Attachment, Theory, Research and Clinical Applications*. 2nd edn (New York: Guilford Press): pp. 552–598

Hodges, J., Steele, M., Hillman, S., Henderson, K. and Kaniuk, J. (2003) 'Changes in Attachment Representations over the First Year of Adoptive Placement: Narratives of Maltreated Children', *Clinical Child Psychology and Psychiatry*, 8 (3): pp. 351–367

Holland, S. (2010) *Child and Family Assessment in Social Work Practice* (London: Sage Publications)

Holmes, J. (2001) *The Search for the Secure Base: Attachment Theory and Psychotherapy* (New York: Routledge)

Holmes, J. and Holmes, J. (2014) *John Bowlby and Attachment Theory*. 2nd edn (London: Routledge)

Howe, D. (2005) *Child Abuse and Neglect: Attachment, Development and Intervention* (London: Palgrave)

Howe, D. (2006) 'Disabled Children, Parent–Child Interaction and Attachment', *Child and Family Social Work*, 11 (2): pp. 95–106

Imamoğlu, S. and Imamoğlu, E. (2006) 'Relationship between General and Context-specific Attachment Orientations in a Turkish Sample', *Journal of Social Psychology*, 146: pp. 261–274, doi: 10.3200/SOCP.146.3.261–274

Insel, T. and Young, L. (2001) 'The Neurobiology of Attachment', *Nature Reviews*, 2: pp. 129–136

Jacobvitz, D., Curran, M. and Moller, N. (2002) 'Measure of Adult Attachment: The Place of Self-report and Interview Methodologies', *Attachment and Human Development*, 4 (2): pp. 207–215

Jenson, J. and Fraser, M. (2010) *Social Policy for Children and Families: A Risk and Resilience Perspective.* 2nd edn (London: SAGE Publications)

Juffer, F., Bakermans-Kranenburg, M. and van IJzendoorn, M. (2008) *Promoting Positive Parenting: An Attachment-based Intervention* (New York: Lawrence Erlbaum Associates)

Karavasillis, L., Doyle, A. and Markiewicz, D. (2003) 'Associations between Parenting Style and Attachment to Mother in Middle Childhood and Adolescence', *International Journal of Behavioral Development*, 27 (2): pp. 153–164

Keller, H. (2013) 'Attachment and Culture', *Journal of Cross-Cultural Psychology*, 44: pp. 175–194

Kerns, K., Schlegelmilch, A., Morgan, T. and Abraham, M. (2005) 'Assessing Attachment in Middle Childhood' in K. Kerns and R. Richardson (eds), *Attachment in Middle Childhood* (New York: Guilford Press): pp. 45–70

Kobak, R. and Madsen, S. (2008) 'Disruptions in Attachment Bonds, Implications for Theory, Research, and Clinical Interventions' in J. Cassidy and P. Shaver (eds), *Handbook of Attachment: Theory, Research and Clinical Implications.* 2nd edn (London: Guilford Press)

Kosciejew, R. (2013) *Object Relations Theory* (Bloomington, IN: Author-House)

Lanyado, M. (2003) 'The Emotional Tasks of Moving from Fostering to Adoption: Transitions, Attachment, Separation and Loss', *Clinical Child Psychology and Psychiatry*, 8 (3): pp. 337–349

Laraeu, A. (2002) 'Invisible Inequality: Social Class and Childrearing in Black Families and White Families', *American Sociological Review*, 67 (5): pp. 747–776

Liotti, G. (2004) 'Trauma, Dissociation, and Disorganization: Three Strands of a Single Braid', *Psychotherapy: Theory, Research, Practice, Training*, 41 (x): pp. 472–486

Lyons-Ruth, K. and Jacobvitz, D. (2008) 'Attachment Disorganisation: Genetic Factors, Parenting Contexts, and Developmental Transformation from Infancy to Adulthood' in *Handbook of Attachment: Theory, Research and Clinical Applications* (London: Guilford Press): pp. 666–697

Lyons-Ruth, K., Yellin, C., Melnick, S. and Atwood, G. (2003) 'Childhood Experiences of Trauma and Loss Have Different Relations to Maternal Unresolved and Hostile-Helpless States of Mind on the AAI', *Attachment and Human Development*, 5 (4): pp. 330–414

Madigan, S., Bakermans-Kranenburg, M., van IJzendoorn, M., Moran, G., Pederson, D. and Benoit, D. (2006) 'Unresolved States of Mind, Anomalous Parental Behavior, and Disorganized Attachment: A Review and Meta-analysis of a Transmission Gap', *Attachment and Human Development*, 8 (2): pp. 89–111

Main, M. (2000) 'The Organized Categories of Infant, Child, and Adult Attachment: Flexible vs. Inflexible Attention under Attachment-related Stress', *Journal of the American Psychoanalytic Association*, 41 (suppl.): pp. 209–244

Main, M. and Hesse, E. (2000) 'Disorganized Infant, Child and Adult Attachment: Collapse in Behavioral and Attentional Strategies', *Journal of American Psychoanalytic Association*, 48 (4): pp. 1097–1127

Main, M. and Weston, D. (1981) 'The Quality of the Toddler's Relationship to Mother and to Father: Related to Conflict Behavior and the Readiness to Establish New Relationships', *Child Development*, 52 (3): pp. 932–940

Marriner, P., Caciolli, J. and Moore, K. (2014) 'The Relationship of Attachment to Resilience and Their Impact on Perceived Stress', in K. Kaniasty, K. Moore, S. Howard and P. Buchwald (eds), *Stress and Anxiety* (Berlin: Logos Verlag): pp. 73–82

Marvin, R. and Pianta, R. (1996) 'Mother's Reactions to Their Child's Diagnosis: Relations with Security of Attachment', *Journal of Clinical Child Psychology*, 25 (4): pp. 436–445

McCarthy, G. and Taylor, A. (1999) 'Avoidant/Ambivalent Attachment Style as a Mediator between Abusive Childhood Experiences and Adult Relationship Difficulties', *Journal of Child Psychology and Psychiatry*, 40 (3): pp. 465–477

McCluskey, U., Hooper, C. A. and Miller, L. (1999) 'Goal-corrected Empathic Attunement: Developing and Rating the Concept within an Attachment Perspective', *Psychotherapy: Theory, Research, Practice, Training*, 36 (1): pp. 80–90

Meins, E. (2013) 'Sensitive Attunement to Infants' Internal States: Operationalizing the Construct of Mind-mindedness', *Attachment and Human Development*, 15 (5–6): pp. 524–544

Mercer, J., Sarner, L. and Rosa, L. (2003) *Attachment Therapy on Trial: The Torture and Death of Candace Newmaker* (Westport, CT: Praeger Publishers)

Mikulincer, M. and Goodman, G. (eds) (2006) *Dynamics of Romantic Love: Attachment, Caregiving and Sex* (New York: Guilford Press)

Mikulincer, M. and Shaver, P. (2012) 'An Attachment Perspective on Psychopathology', *World Psychiatry*, 11 (1): pp. 11–15

Milyavskaya, M. and Lyndon, J. (2013) 'Strong but Insecure: Examining the Prevalence and Correlates of Insecure Attachment Bonds with Attachment Figures', *Journal of Social and Personal Relationships*, 30 (5): pp. 529–544

Music, G. (2010) *Nurturing Natures: Attachment and Childhood Emotion* (Abingdon: Psychology Press)

O'Connor, T. and Byrne, J. (2007) 'Attachment Measures for Research and Practice', *Child and Adolescent Mental Health*, 12 (4): pp. 187–192

Ontai, L. and Thompson, A. (2008) 'Attachment, Parent–Child Discourse and Theory-of-Mind Development', *Social Development*, 17 (1): pp. 47–60

Out, D., Bakermans-Kranenburg, M. and van IJzendoorn, M. (2009) 'The Role of Disconnected and Extremely Insensitive Parenting in the Development of Disorganized Attachment: The Validation of a New Measure', *Attachment and Human Development*, 11 (5): pp. 419–443

Owens, E. and Shaw, D. (2003) 'Poverty and Early Childhood Adjustment', in S. Luthar (ed.), *Resilience and Vulnerability: Adaptation in the Context of Childhood Adversities* (Cambridge: Cambridge University Press): pp. 267–292

Padrón, E., Carlson, E. A. and Sroufe, L. A. (2014) 'Frightened Versus Not Frightened Disorganized Infant Attachment: Newborn Characteristics and Maternal Caregiving', *American Journal of Orthopsychiatry*, 84 (2), pp. 201–208

Palm, G. (2014) 'Attachment Theory and Fathers: Moving from "Being There" to "Being With"', *Journal of Family Theory and Review*, doi: 10.1111/jftr.12045

Parkes, C. M. (2006) *Love and Loss: The Roots of Grief and Its Complications* (London: Routledge)

Pearson, J. (1994) 'Earned- and Continuous-Security in Adult Attachment: Relation to Depressive Symptomatology and Parenting Style', *Development and Psychopathology*, 6 (2): pp. 359–373

Pietromonaco, P., DeBuse, C. and Powers, S. (2013) 'Does Attachment Get under the Skin? Adult Romantic Attachment and Cortisol Responses to Stress', *Current Directions in Psychological Science*, 22 (1): pp. 63–68

Pinker, S. (2003) *The Blank Slate: The Modern Denial of Human Nature* (London: Penguin)

Pocock, D. (2010) 'Debating Truth, Error and Distortion in Systemic Psychotherapy. A Contribution from the DMM'. Available at http://www.patcrittenden.com/include/docs/dmm_context_pocock.pdf

Prior, V. and Glaser, D. (2006) *Understanding Attachment and Attachment Disorders: Theory, Evidence and Practice* (London: Jessica Kingsley Publishers)

Rassin, E. and van Rootselaar, A. (2006) 'From Dissociation to Trauma? Individual Differences in Dissociation as Predictor of 'Trauma' Perception', *Journal of Behavior Therapy and Experimental Psychiatry*, 37 (2): pp. 127–139

Ravitz, P., Maunder, R., Hunter, J., Sthankiya, B. and Lancee, W. (2010) 'Adult Attachment Measures: A 25-Year Review', *Journal of Psychosomatic Research*, 69 (4): pp. 419–432

Read, J. and Bentall, J. (2012) 'Negative Childhood Experiences and Mental Health: Theoretical, Clinical and Primary Prevention Implications', *The British Journal of Psychiatry*, 200 (2): pp. 89–91

Redshaw, M. and Martin, C. (2013) 'Babies, "bonding" and Ideas about Parental "Attachment"', *Journal of Reproductive and Infant Psychology*, doi: 10.1080/02646838.2013.830383

Riggs, S. and Riggs, D. (2011) 'Risk and Resilience in Military Families Experiencing Deployment: The Role of the Family Attachment Network', *Journal of Family Psychology*, 25 (5): pp. 675–687

Rholes, S., Simpson, J. and Friedman, M. (2006) 'Avoidant Attachment and the Experience of Parenting', *Personality and Social Psychology Bulletin*, 32 (3): pp. 275–285

Rilling, J. (2009) 'A Potential Role for Oxytocin in the Intergenerational Transmission of Secure Attachment', *Neuropsychopharmacology*, 34 (13): pp. 2621–2622

Robert, M. (2009) 'Trauma and Dismissing (Avoidant) Attachment: Intervention Strategies in Individual Psychotherapy', *Psychotherapy: Theory, Research, Practice, Training*, 46 (1): pp. 68–81

Roisman, G., Padron, E., Sroufe, L. A. and Egeland, B. (2002) 'Earned-Secure Attachment Status in Retrospect and Prospect', *Child Development*, 73 (4): pp. 1204–1219

Rutter, M. (1979) 'Maternal Deprivation, 1972–78: New Findings, New Concepts, New Approaches', *Child Development*, 50 (2): pp. 283–305

Schmitt, D. (2003) 'Are Men Universally More Dismissing Than Women? Gender Differences in Romantic Attachment across 62 Cultural Regions', *Personal Relationships*, 10 (3): pp. 307–331

Scott, K., Kim, Y., Nolf, K., Hallquist, M., Wright, A., Stepp, S., Morse, J. and Pilkonis, P. (2013) 'Preoccupied Attachment and Emotional Dysregulation: Specific Aspects of Borderline Personality Disorder or General Dimensions of Personality Pathology?', *Journal of Personality Disorders*, 27 (4): pp. 473–495, doi: 10.1521/pedi_2013_27_099

Seay, B. and Harlow, H. (1965) 'Maternal Separation in the Rhesus Monkey', *Journal of Nervous and Mental Diseases*, 140 (6): pp. 434–441

Sethre-Hofstad, L., Stansbury, K. and Rice, M. (2002) 'Attunement of Maternal and Child Adrenocortical Response to Child Challenge', *Psychoneuroendocrinology*, 27 (6): pp. 731–747

Shaver, P. and Fraley, R. C. (2006) 'Attachment, Loss and Grief: Bowlby's Views and Current Controversies', in J. Cassidy and P. Shaver (eds), *Handbook of Attachment: Theory, Research and Clinical Implications*. 2nd edn (London: Guilford Press): pp. 48–77

Shaw, C., Brodie, I., Ellis, A., Graham, B., Mainey, A., de Sousa, S. and Willmott, N. (2010) *Research into Private Fostering* (London: Department for Children, Schools and Families)

Shemmings, D. (2006) 'Using Adult Attachment Theory to Differentiate Adult Children's Internal Working Models of Later Life Filial Relationships', *Journal of Aging Studies*, 20 (2) (April): pp. 177–191

Shemmings, D. (2014) 'Disorganised Attachment and Reactive Attachment Disorders' in P. Holmes and S. Farnfield (eds), *The Routledge Handbook of Attachment (Vol 1: Theory)* (London: Routledge)

Shemmings, D. and Shemmings, Y. (2011) *Understanding Disorganized Attachment: Theory and Practice for Working with Children and Adults* (London: Jessica Kingsley Publishers)

Shemmings, D. and Shemmings, Y. (eds) (2014) *Assessing Disorganized Attachment Behaviour in Children: An Evidence-based Model for Understanding and Supporting Families* (London: Jessica Kingsley Publishers)

Shirley, M. (1942) 'Children's Adjustments to a Strange Situation', *The Journal of Abnormal and Social Psychology*, 37 (2): pp. 201–217

Shmueli-Goetz, Y., Target, M., Fonagy, P. and Datta, A. (2008) 'The Child Attachment Interview: A Psychometric Study of Reliability and Discriminant Validity', *Developmental Psychology*, 44 (4): pp. 939–956

Shore, J. and Shore, A. (2008) 'Modern Attachment Theory: The Central Role of Affect Regulation in Development and Treatment', *Clinical Social Work Journal*, 36 (1): pp. 9–20

Silver, M. (2013) *Attachment in Common Sense and Doodle: A Practice Guide* (London: Jessica Kingsley Publishers)

Simpson, J. and Belsky, J. (2006) 'Attachment Theory within a Modern Evolutionary Framework' in J. Cassidy and P. Shaver (eds), *Handbook of Attachment: Theory, Research and Clinical Implications*. 2nd edn (London: Guilford Press): pp. 131–157

Slade, A. (2005) 'Parental Reflective Functioning: An Introduction', *Attachment and Human Development*, 7 (3): pp. 269–281

Sroufe, L. A. (1995) *Emotional Development: The Organization of Emotional Life in the Early Years* (New York: Cambridge University Press)

Sroufe, L. A. (2005) 'Attachment and Development: A Prospective, Longitudinal Study from Birth to Adulthood', *Attachment and Human Development*, 7 (4): pp. 349–367

Sroufe, L. A., Carlson, E., Levy, A. and Egeland, B. (1999) 'Implications of Attachment Theory for Developmental Psychopathology', *Development and Psychopathology*, 11 (1): pp. 1–13

Steele, H., Steele, M. and Fonagy, P. (1996) 'Associations among Attachment Classifications of Mothers, Fathers and Their Infants', *Child Development*, 67 (2): pp. 541–555

Steele, M., Steele, H., Woolgar, M., Yabsley, S., Fonagy, P., Johnson, D. and Croft, C. (2003) 'An Attachment Perspective on Children's Emotion Narratives: Links across Generations' in R. Emde, D. Wolf and D. Oppenheim (eds), *Revealing the Inner Worlds of Young Children: The MacArthur Story Stem Battery and Parent–Child Narratives* (New York: Oxford University Press): pp. 163–181

Stern, M., Karraker, K., Sopko, A. and Norman, S. (2000) 'The Prematurity Stereotype Revisited: Impact on Mother-Fullterm and Mother-Premature Infant Interactions', *Infant Mental Health Journal*, 21 (6): pp. 495–509

Stoltenborgh, M., Bakermans-Kranenburg, M. and van IJzendoorn, M. (2013) 'The Neglect of Child Neglect: A Meta-analytic Review of the Prevalence of Neglect', *Social Psychiatry and Psychiatric Epidemiology*, 48 (3): pp. 345–355

Stovall-McClough, K. and Dozier, M. (2004) 'Forming Attachments in Foster Care: Infant Attachment Behaviors during the First 2 Months of Placement', *Development and Psychopathology*, 16 (2): pp. 253–271

Stronach, E., Toth, S., Rogosch, F., Oshri, A., Manly, J. and Cicchetti, D. (2011) 'Child Maltreatment, Attachment Security, and Internal Representations of Mother and Mother–Child Relationships', *Child Maltreatment*, 16 (2): pp. 137–145

Tarabulsy, G., Bernier, A., Provost, M., Maranda, J., Larose, S., Moss, E., Larose, M. and Terrier, R. (2005) 'Another Look Inside the Gap: Ecological Contributions to the Transmission of Attachment in a Sample of Adolescent Mother–Infant Dyads', *Developmental Psychology*, 41 (1): pp. 212–224

Target, M., Fonagy, P. and Shmueli-Goetz, Y. (2003) 'Attachment Representations in School-Age Children: The Development of the Child Attachment Interview (CAI)', *Journal of Child Psychotherapy*, 29 (2): pp. 171–186

Tarren-Sweeney, M. (2013) 'An Investigation of Complex Attachment- and Trauma-related Symptomology among Children in Foster and Kinship Care', *Child Psychiatry and Human Development*, 44 (6): pp. 727–741

Thompson, R. (1994) 'Emotion Regulation: A Theme in Search of a Definition' in N. Fox (ed.) 'The Development of Emotion Regulation: Biological and Behavioural Considerations', *Monographs of the Society for Research in Child Development*, 59 (2–3): pp. 225–252

Thompson, R. and Madigan, S. (2005) *Memory: The Key to Consciousness* (New Jersey: Princeton University Press)

Turner, P. (1991) 'Relations between Attachment, Gender, and Behavior with Peers in Preschool', *Child Development*, 62 (6): pp. 1475–1488

Van den Dries, L., Juffer, F., van IJzendoorn, M. and Bakermans-Kranenburg, M. (2009) 'Fostering Security? A Meta-analysis of

Attachment in Adopted Children', *Children and Youth Services Review*, 31 (3): pp. 410–421

Van Dijken, S. (1998) *John Bowlby: His Early Life, A Biographical Journey into the Roots of Attachment Theory* (London: Free Association Books)

van IJzendoorn, M., Bakermans-Kranenburg, M. and Marian, J. (1997) 'Intergenerational Transmission of Attachment: A Move to the Contextual Level' in L. Atkinson and K. Zucker (eds), *Attachment and Psychopathology* (New York: Guilford Press): pp. 135–170

van IJzendoorn, M. and De Wolff, M. (1997) 'In Search of Absent Father – Meta-analyses of Infant–Father Attachment: A Rejoinder to Our Discussants', *Child Development*, 68 (4): pp. 604–609

van IJzendoorn, M., Juffer, F. and Duyvesteyn, M. (1995) 'Breaking the Intergenerational Cycle of Insecure Attachment', *Journal of Child Psychology and Psychiatry*, 36 (2): pp. 225–248

van IJzendoorn, M. and Kroonenberg, P. (1988) 'Cross-cultural Patterns of Attachment: A Meta-analysis of the Strange Situation', *Child Development*, 59 (1): pp. 147–156

van IJzendoorn, M. and Sagi, A. (1999) 'Cross-cultural Patterns of Attachment: Universal and Contextual Dimensions' in J. Cassidy and P. Shaver (eds), *Handbook of Attachment* (New York: Guilford Press)

Vaughn, B., Bost, K. and van IJzendoorn, M. (2008) 'Attachment and Temperament: Additive and Interactive Influences on Behavior, Affect, and Cognition during Infancy and Childhood' in J. Cassidy and P. Shaver (eds), *The Handbook of Attachment: Theory, Research and Clinical Applications.* 2nd edn (New York: Guilford Press): pp. 192–216

Walker, J. (2008) 'Guide to Unresolved Trauma in Parents and Its Implications in Terms of Child Protection', *Community Care Inform.* Available at http://www.ccinform.co.uk/guides/guide-to-unresolved-trauma-in-parents-and-its-implications-in-terms-of-child-protection/

Walsh, J. (2009) 'Children's Understandings of Mental Ill Health: Implications for Risk and Resilience in Relationships', *Child and Family Social Work*, 14 (1): pp. 115–122

Ward, H. and Brown, R. (2013) 'Decision-making within a Child's Timeframe: A Response', *Family Law* (September): pp. 1181–1186

Waters, E., Crowell, J., Elliott, M., Corcoran, D. and Treboux, D. (2002) 'Bowlby's Secure Base Theory and the Social/Personality Psychology of Attachment patterns: Work(s) in Progress', *Attachment and Human Development*, 4 (2): pp. 230–242

Waters, E. and Cummings, M. (2000) 'A Secure Base from Which to Explore Close Relationships', *Child Development*, 71 (1): pp. 164–172

Waters, E. and McIntosh, J. (2011) 'Are We Asking the Right Questions about Attachment?' *Family Court Review*, 49 (3): pp. 474–482

Waters, E., Merrick, S., Treboux, D., Crowell, J. and Albersheim, L. (2000) 'Attachment Security in Infancy and Early Childhood: A Twenty-One Longitudinal Study', *Child Development*, 71 (3): pp. 684–689

Weiss, Y. and Shilkret, R. (2010) 'The Importance of the Peer Group in the Israeli Kibbutz for Adult Attachment Pattern', *Smith College Studies in Social Work*, 80 (1): pp. 2–19

Wellman, H., Cross, D. and Watson, J. (2001) 'Meta-analysis of Theory-of-Mind Development: The Truth about False Belief', *Journal of Child Development*, 72 (3): pp. 655–684

White, S. and Wastell, D. (unpublished, 2013) 'A Response to Brown, R. and Ward, H. "Decision-making within the Child's Timeframe"'. Available at http://www.14gis.co.uk/documents/Response_to_Brown_and_Ward_17th_June.pdf. Accessed September 2013

Wimmer, H. and Perner, J. (1983) 'Beliefs about Beliefs: Representation and Constraining Function of Wrong Beliefs in Young Children's Understanding of Deception', *Journal of Cognition*, 13 (1): pp. 103–128

Winnicott, D. (1956) 'Primary Maternal Preoccupation' in *Through Paediatrics to Psychoanalysis* (London: Hogarth)

Winnicott, D. (1992) *The Child, The Family and the Outside World*. 2nd edn (New York: Perseus Publishing)

Woolgar, M. and Scott, S. (2013) 'The Negative Consequences of Over-diagnosing Attachment Disorders in Adopted Children: The Importance of Comprehensive Formulations', *Clinical Child Psychology and Psychiatry*, 19 (3): pp. 355–366

index